RESEARCH IN SOCIAL ANTHRO

an SSRC review of current research

SOCIAL SCIENCE RESEARCH COUNCIL

Reviews of Current Research

Research in
Social Anthropology

HEINEMANN
LONDON

Heinemann Educational Books Ltd
LONDON   MELBOURNE   TORONTO
SINGAPORE   JOHANNESBURG
AUCKLAND   IBADAN
NAIROBI   HONG KONG

ISBN 435 82842 8

(c

Published by Heinemann Educational Books Ltd
48 Charles Street, London W.1
for the Social Science Research Council
State House, High Holborn, London W.C.1
Printed in Great Britain by
Morrison and Gibb Ltd
London and Edinburgh

Contents

CONTENTS

SOME RECENT BRITISH WORK IN SOCIAL
ANTHROPOLOGY

FOREWORD

This is one of a series of reviews, prepared under the auspices of the Social Science Research Council (SSRC), which deals with various aspects of research in the social sciences.

One of the SSRC's main reasons for sponsoring the preparation of these reviews is to get the views of some of the leading research workers in the field about important current research developments, about likely future developments and about the research needs of the subject, in terms of men, money, other resources and research organization.

As well as helping to guide the SSRC in its future policy, the research reviews will, at a time when there is increasing specialization within all social science disciplines, help social scientists and students to keep abreast of developments over a wider field.

The reviews will also provide those in industry, government, the educational world and elsewhere with information about recent developments in the social sciences.

The research reviews are prepared in different ways. Some are drawn up by Committees of the Council, others by *ad hoc* panels of specialists brought together with the sole aim of compiling a review. Some deal with a particular social science discipline, others with a problem or range of problems involving a number of disciplines. The reviews do not therefore follow any standardized pattern, and the groups involved in preparing them are free to tackle them in whatever ways they think are appropriate.

Some social science disciplines and problems may not be susceptible to this kind of approach, and so this series of reviews does not aim to provide a comprehensive picture of everything that is going on in all the social sciences. It should also be stressed that the reviews are in no sense formal policy statements by the SSRC —their function is to inform.

JEREMY MITCHELL, *series editor*

ACKNOWLEDGEMENTS

This review of research has been based on the material provided by members of the Social Anthropology Committee of the SSRC, whose names are listed on p. ix, and by E. W. Ardener, Lorraine Barič, Burton Benedict, J. K. C. Campbell, Daryll Forde, J. A. W. Forge, Maurice Freedman, J. R. Goody, I. M. Lewis, J. Littlejohn, D. Maybury-Lewis, M. G. Smith, and I. R. Whittaker. The Committee is very grateful to those who have helped by providing data papers, and also to those many members of the Association of Social Anthropologists who supplied information about their research activities. The Committee is also much indebted to I. M. Lewis, who analysed the research data supplied. Helpful comments were made on the draft review by the Chairman and members of the SSRC, but the views expressed in this Review are those of the Committee alone.

RAYMOND FIRTH
Chairman, Social Anthropology Committee, SSRC

MEMBERSHIP OF SSRC
COMMITTEE ON SOCIAL ANTHROPOLOGY

PROFESSOR R. W. FIRTH, *Department of Anthropology, London School of Economics and Political Science* (*chairman*)

PROFESSOR F. G. BAILEY, *Department of Social Anthropology, University of Sussex*

PROFESSOR M. P. BANTON,[2] *Department of Sociology, University of Bristol*

DR J. H. M. BEATTIE,[1] *Institute of Social Anthropology, University of Oxford*

MR M. CHISHOLM,[1] *Department of Geography, University of Bristol*

PROFESSOR H. M. GLUCKMAN, *Department of Social Anthropology, University of Manchester*

DR E. R. LEACH, *Department of Anthropology, University of Cambridge*

PROFESSOR K. L. LITTLE, *Department of Social Anthropology, University of Edinburgh*

DR J. B. LOUDON,[1] *Department of Sociology and Anthropology, University College of Swansea*

PROFESSOR A. C. MAYER,[1] *Department of Asian Anthropology, School of Oriental and African Studies, University of London*

PROFESSOR T. H. MARSHALL,[2] *Professor Emeritus, Department of Sociology, London School of Economics and Political Science*

[1] Joined Committee after this review was prepared.
[2] Member of Committee at the time this review was prepared, but has since ceased membership.

1 Scope and Method of Research

General

Social anthropology is one of the more recently developed sciences of man. Grown during the last half century out of broad comparative studies of ethnography and ethnology, concerned with the worldwide description of customs and institutions and the evolutionary and historical relations between very different social forms, social anthropology has also been inspired by and contributed to the development of sociological theory.

Basically, the study is concerned with problems of how societies or communities are composed, how they operate as wholes and in their several parts, how they change, and what relation individual and group choice and action have to the rules and practices provided by the conditions of social living. Whether it is whole communities or single institutions of complex societies that are studied, their structure and functions are considered in this total context. But while in such study social anthropology is closely related to sociology, it has a tradition and methods of its own which continue to distinguish it as a separate discipline.

The tradition of social anthropology is broadly one of *integrative, comparative* and *observational* study of human behaviour in its social context.

It is *integrative* because every attempt is made to see social behaviour 'in the round'. A study of marriage, for example, examines not only who marries whom, the legal rules and ritual customs involved, the conditions of choice for spouses and the domestic relations between them; it also considers how the union is affected by the economic transfers that are commonly required, and by the implications for group linkage, social status, and the rights over any children that may be born. The focus of the study is integrative in that the

1

aim is to see the bearing which any part of the action may have on any other. This does not mean that social anthropologists regard all institutions in society as well-adjusted. They look for evidence of conflict, and recognize that radical contradiction of principle may be of great social significance. But systematic study of possible functional relationships of an institution is necessary to bring out the degree of harmony or conflict involved. While the 'structural/functional' approach has been broadened and modified in recent years, it is still characteristic of most research in the subject.

Social anthropology is *comparative* because a study of any one type of institution, say, a particular form of marriage, is made implicitly against the background of the range of marriage types known over all human societies. So a study such as that of polygyny (plural wives) in Muslim society is not only made in terms of the economic, social, moral, ritual, and political variables involved, but also seen in perspective, by implicit or explicit comparison with practices of polygyny in other societies with different social structures, economic levels, religious and moral ideas about the relative positions of men and women. So the generalizations of social anthropology are formulated and tested by reference to a range of data drawn from many societies, from the most 'simple' or 'underdeveloped' (formerly often called 'primitive' in reference to their lack of complex technology) to the most sophisticated. It is this comparative perspective on problems such as those of family and marriage, the position of women, kinship, chieftainship and kingship, ritual and religion, ideas about the nature of man and his relation to the world around him, that enables social anthropology to make its proper contribution to the social sciences.

Social anthropology is an *observational* study because it lays a major stress upon the need to get direct first-hand evidence of social relationships. It uses questionnaires and other structured interview methods to obtain data about social attitudes and social behaviour, and such methods can be usefully developed for quantitative analysis. But a prime concern of the social anthropologist is not only with what men say and with what they say they do, but also with what they can be seen to do. In the anthropological view there is no substitute for results obtained by direct observation. This does not mean a crude empiricism. It is recognized that direct observation must be infused with theory and guided by hypotheses. But an outcome of this concern with empirical observation is the emphasis laid upon intensive methods of field research.

Field research in other societies is a vital means of acquiring data in social anthropology. In the earlier history of the subject such material came from documentary sources —information provided by explorers, missionaries, government officials. But the efficient development of the discipline has rested upon the fact that over the last half-century social anthropologists themselves, equipped with the requisite theoretical training, have engaged in long periods of collection of original data in the field. Living among the people they study, speaking the vernacular language, attending the marriage ceremonies, feasts and funerals, forming relations of confidence and friendship, anthropologists have been able to give their data a validity which it would be difficult or even impossible to secure otherwise. Some anthropologists have made repeated studies of the same community at different periods of time, or carried out studies in two or more communities of different environment and social conditions. Material from such studies has been invaluable in the construction of comparative generalizations and the general development of the theory of the subject. It also provides a very salutary standpoint from which to observe and analyse the institutions of the anthropologist's own society.

Field research in other countries is necessary also to secure the proper training of social anthropologists. This is not merely a matter of placing a student in an appropriate field situation and controlling his collection of the data relevant to his problem. A more subtle principle is involved. The hallmark of fieldwork in social anthropology is often said to be 'participant observation'. Few social anthropologists have claimed that they ever were treated precisely as members of the community in which they studied; identity of interest and behaviour is not at issue. But the fieldworker's partial absorption into the life of the community is a most significant element in his research. It means that he is not only 'getting to know' the people he is studying; he is also necessarily conforming to a considerable degree to their values. In taking part in their ceremonies, their exchanges, their discussions of spirits and other mystical concepts, the anthropologists must adopt a kind of 'as if' manner, giving sufficient credence to the people's ideas to allow him to move freely among them and share their actions. By subjecting himself to the standards of another society the anthropologist inevitably—and sometimes quite overtly—is forced to reconsider his own.

The perspective resulting from this confrontation of values is a major factor in the contribution of social anthropology to comparative studies. The view that field research is treated as a kind of initiation by social anthropologists has more than a superficial significance. The fact that not all social anthropologists engage in fieldwork, and not all of those who do fieldwork in fact go into other communities than their own, does not invalidate these propositions; the tradition of the discipline has been formed through the experience of the major part of its members.

One corollary of this 'cross-cultural' perspective is that a social anthropologist is not expected to be committed from the outset to any moral position in the evaluation of any institutions he is studying. He may have personal views as to its value, but his job in the first instance is to lay bare its relationships and effects upon the people concerned and in the society at large. So it is no accident that social anthropologists were among the first to issue systematic, dispassionate studies of topics such as polygamy, pre-marital sex behaviour, incest, abortion, infanticide, suicide, and homicide, which are now recognized as needing such scientific consideration if social action upon them is to be firmly based.

Relations with other disciplines

Refinements in social anthropology and rapidly changing conditions in the modern world have brought into greater relief the relation of the subject with other disciplines concerned with the examination of social behaviour. With sociology there is an increased sharing of the field, both empirical and theoretical, which has led to a few demarcation problems, but has also meant very fruitful reciprocal borrowing and co-operation. Social anthropology was for long unconcerned with economics and politics, but in recent years relations between them have developed in interesting ways. Changing conditions in most communities studied have brought home to social anthropologists the need for a broader frame of theory than that which they were able to use when these communities were still in a relatively underdeveloped state. Conversely as economists and students of government have been increasingly attracted by problems of economic growth and political self-determination in countries overseas, the knowledge possessed by social anthropologists of the institutions and values of the people of these countries has become of interest to some of them. Economic growth has not always followed according to plan, and the setting up of 'democratic' forms of government sometimes had unexpected results. Analyses by social anthropologists at the 'grass roots' level have sometimes been able to throw light upon unsuspected complications. Studies in economic anthropology and political anthropology have now become common, and joint work by social anthropologists with economists or

5

political scientists has begun to appear. Many of these studies have obvious application to practical problems. Investigations of the relation of ecological factors to economic and political organization, e.g. in farming economies, have also had an interest, both applied and theoretical. Anthropological research on systems of law, especially tribal systems, drawing on the concepts and modes of analysis of Euro-American jurisprudence, has made an increasingly significant contribution to the comparative study of law. Understanding of the basic nature of law and of processes of social control, both in instituted courts and in the ordinary affairs of life, has also been promoted by such research as is evidenced by the use of such studies by legal scholars. In this legal field the studies of anthropologists have obvious relevance to the interpretation of the economic and political future of developing nations.

Some of the more difficult problems in the relation of social anthropology to other studies of man appear with linguistics and with psychology. Both linguistics and psychology in recent years have developed a highly technical theoretical framework, much of which, like that of economics, seems to have little application to the problems of anthropology. Yet, in each discipline, precise, systematic methods of study and generalizations about human behaviour have a bearing upon much of the work of social anthropologists. Processes of choice and decision-making, the structural complications of the language of kinship, or the principles of thought which underlie the diverse cognitive systems identified in myth, are all examples of areas where social anthropology can contribute to and draw upon the work of these other disciplines.

Modern position of social anthropology
Traditionally, social anthropology has been the scientific study of exotic custom, and in the popular view this is what it still largely is. This view is erroneous.

A quarter of a century ago it was still fairly novel for a British social anthropologist to study a peasant society of developed character, but even then there were investigations of Mexican markets, the economics of Malay fishermen and their wives and, in more historical vein, the growth of the Sanusiya Order among Beduin of Cyrenaica. At the same time as technical changes, with economic and political developments, radically modified the former tribal societies, anthropologists too widened their range of problems and altered their approach. They studied people who grew crops for sale, entered the industrial labour market, participated increasingly in local and national structures of government and who, in so doing, developed new forms of leadership, new family problems, and new religious cults.

In such studies anthropologists have come more and more to see the relevance of giving a broad dimension to the problems they investigate; book titles such as *New Nations* (51)[1] or *Tribe, Caste and Nation* (9) illustrate this trend. But the modernization which is transforming the traditional types of society does not do away with the segments of local life. In rural areas, as Bailey has stated for India, the village 'remains an arena within which individuals struggle with one another for power' and often also for land and other resources. In urban areas the struggle is of another order, but co-operation and competition still go on in workshop, neighbourhood or household. It is above all at this 'grass roots' or 'cement floor' level of observation and analysis of social relationships that the contribution of the anthropologist is most marked, and distinguishes his kind of study in general from those of other social scientists.

It is clear that as social, economic, and political conditions change in societies all over the world, the subject-matter for

---

[1] Figures in parenthesis refer to the publications mentioned in the note on some recent British work in social anthropology on p. 106.

the study does not vanish; the problems for social anthropology becomes more, not less numerous.

This applies also to the interest of social anthropology in Western, including British, society. Historically, anthropological studies in Britain, ethnographic as well as physical, go back well into the nineteenth century, though it is only about twenty years since British social anthropologists turned their attention at all systematically to investigations in their own society. But now, enquiries into family and kin relations, the social life of villages and housing estates, elements in the organization of factory work, local politics, race relations, the social background to health problems, are examples of the application of anthropological methods of research to current problems in our own society.

There is a further point of fundamental importance for an understanding of the anthropological position. The scientist works always in a frame of implicit comparative concepts. Social anthropologists do not regard Western institutions, beliefs, and codes of behaviour as self-sufficient objects of study; but endeavour to set them in the perspective of a more general set of social forms. As social anthropology develops, then, the evidence from Western societies can be increasingly set alongside that from other societies in any part of the world.

There are some differences of view as to what this implies for the classification of social anthropology. Worldwide changes in political structure, with the attainment of independence by many formerly dependent territories, has led a few social anthropologists to emphasize the 'de-colonization' phase of anthropology, and to regard the subject as primarily either a chronicler of the past or sociology under another name. But most other social anthropologists have begun to stress even more than before the broad comparative nature of their discipline, and to concern themselves more overtly with basic problems of human thought and behaviour over a worldwide range. They find links with physical anthropologists, animal ethologists, linguists, and other scientists interested at the greatest level of generality in the most refined studies of the character and actions of man in social conditions. This trend has led to an opinion that social anthropology in some respects is becoming not more but less sociological. Such differences of view, based upon a combination of personal temperament and perception of significant problems capable of development, are a sign of the vitality and power of adaptation of the study to new conditions.

2 Current Research Themes

Social structure
Much of the traditional subject-matter of social anthropology
can be summed up under the general head of social structure:
marriage, family, kinship, descent groups; social status and
stratification, position of women, rank, caste, class; associations ranging from blood-brotherhood to age grades and
secret societies. Much research has been done under all of
these heads. But anthropologists assume that the rules and
behaviour patterns represented by such topics are not
independent or random, that they are linked in complex ways
in a given universe of social relations, by some regular
arrangement of interdependent parts, with some degree of
continuity over time. Moreover, it has been assumed that the
relation between the various parts of the social structure is of
a functional order, so that any institutional complex tends to
support the whole.

Much attention has been devoted to critical scrutiny of
these concepts which, while pragmatically useful as a stimulus
to field research, are theoretically open to various objections.
In particular, it has been pointed out that conflict in varying
degree may exist between different elements in the social
structure, and between structural forms and the aims of
individual members of the society; and that inconsistencies
amounting to contradiction may inhibit the full realization of
social goals. Studies in property-holding, inheritance, political
process, have brought out important areas of conflict. The
significance of ritualized procedures in providing means of
cathartic expression and resolution of conflict has been
demonstrated.

Recent theoretical discussion of social structure by British
social anthropologists, influenced considerably by the views of
Claude Lévi-Strauss, has tended to focus on the identification

and construction of 'models', and on the use of these for the interpretation of the observed 'reality' of empirical behaviour. Some transactional models in the British tradition have used games-theory of simple form. But most models are derived from what are thought of as elementary principles of social behaviour. They are constructed with what purport to be concrete components, neutrally regarded—women, goods, services. They are activated by the primary dynamic of exchange (i.e. the need to communicate as a basic factor of social existence). It should be pointed out that the anthropological treatment of models has followed a rather different line from that in some other social sciences, e.g. economics. Anthropologists, like economists, have made model constructions of articulated sets of variables and have drawn logical inferences from their assumptions, to explain and to some extent to predict what happens in the 'real' world. But anthropological models can rarely be subjected to quantitative treatment. Again, with anthropologists, model and empirical reality have often tended to become confused. Sometimes the model has been conceived as the 'true' type of behaviour, and the empirical data have been adjusted ('re-interpreted') in the light of it. Models, as the observer's own construct, are said to be 'unconscious' for the people whose behaviour is being examined. But sometimes the position has been complicated by the introduction of an intermediate concept, the 'conscious model' or 'home-made model', which is represented as a people's own ideas about the patterning of that particular institution under study. More refined versions of the 'home-made' models distinguish between the different conceptions of the form and character of their society held by members of different social classes, e.g. a sophisticated literate gentry and an illiterate peasantry.

Where model construction in social anthropology has been most successful so far has been in the fields of kinship, descent grouping, and marriage; political behaviour; and myth. Its main value has been in the isolation of basic principles of social behaviour, in such terms as allow them to be related and combined in ways which do not so much give a plausible explanation of observed behaviour as suggest possible connections for further research.[1]

In the theory of social structure anthropologists have been much concerned with questions of degree of integration and of persistence or change over time. In considering the relation between social rules and sanctions and the behaviour of individual members of a society the concepts of social integration or cohesion, social rigidity and 'strength' or 'weakness' of kin units have been much used. Generalizations have been put forward, for example, relating the prevalence of deviant behaviour such as suicide directly to the degree of rigidity in the institutions of the society. But though useful notions at an early stage of the analysis, these qualities require further elucidation, with more attention to objective measures for determining them. The existence of clearly defined social groups and well-formulated social rules does not necessarily indicate a high degree of 'cohesiveness' in a society. From the point of view of historical continuity, indeed, societies which are 'loosely' structured may have demonstrated as much cohesion as others which are much more clearly articulated.

Increasingly, social anthropologists have been experimenting with approaches which look for correlations outside structure in the narrow sense, in terms either of a sequence of historical events, or of factors of environment, to explain particular social forms. Some have been writing history, not merely, as we are often told, because the tribal reservoirs are drying up, but because they wish to examine, in a field where empirical examination is possible, how structural elements (if not whole structures) respond to factors of change.

---

[1] Among the publications in the list on p. 106 that deal with the use of models in social anthropology are nos. 3, 37 and 41.

Such diachronic studies make it possible to perceive more clearly the relative movement and weighting of factors which are quite crucial to the understanding of the functioning of institutions. Single-dimensional, synchronic analyses are likely to distort fundamentally the perspectives of interpretation. This diachronic approach can be regarded as the most tightly controlled type of comparative analysis. It serves to reveal the multiplicity of functions which, in only slightly different settings, may be served by what appears formally (and culturally) as the same institution. Examples of this method are recent studies of the changing functions, over time, of lineages in Arab border villages in Israel; and of the dynamic quality of conflict in Tonga cults of spirit-possession.

What is studied under the name 'social change' offers special opportunities for an enhanced understanding of the working of institutions, and for testing the validity of particular structural analyses. For if a society has the structure attributed to it at a particular point in time, it should be possible to make valid predictions of the ways in which it will respond to change. At least, it should be possible to understand the new situation as in some meaningful fashion related to the past. Again, since the study is diachronic, we can sift out superficial relationships from deep attachments and correlations between institutional complexes. This has been demonstrated in studies of some modern African and Asian political processes which have been shown to have their roots in the conditions of traditional politics. Modern social conditions involving traditional organizations, as Malinowski rightly diagnosed, provide a laboratory for those who are interested in the empirical study of society.

These 'laboratory' opportunities need to be developed. There is still a poverty of good studies. In the rich field of Africa, for example, there are still too few detailed studies or comparative analyses of urban ethnic associations, of urban

13

tribalism, or urban kinship—and this despite the fact that so much work has been done on social change in Africa.

In the examination of the ecological impact upon social structures Forde's pioneering work of thirty years ago has only recently been followed up. Here American social anthropologists have led the way; for instance Sahlins (1961) has sought to pin-point the ecologically adaptive features of 'predatory lineages'. Other studies by British anthropologists have related agnation—membership of a patrilineal descent group—to population density and availability of resources, and examined the relation between land tenure, rice cultivation, and kinship in Asian communities. A comparative study (supported by the SSRC) is under way in Somalia, designed to elucidate the differential ecological relations of cultivation and of nomadism to the local social structures. Much, however, still remains to be done in this promising field.

Kinship

One primary interest of social anthropological work has been and still is the study of kinship. Intensive research into family structures and into marriage forms continues over a wide range of societies, and the British contribution to the theory of the subject is considerable. Important also has been the analysis and definition of descent systems, especially unilineal structures. In recent years reconsideration of problems connected with lineage structures, especially in Africa, has thrown fresh light on their functions and ideologies. Recent work on double descent systems in West Africa has provided new hypotheses concerning the factors (particularly economic factors) involved in generating and sustaining such systems. Notable here in recent years is the emphasis, in which Cambridge has taken a leading part, on domestic units as well as on descent group units, and on the significance of the developmental cycle whereby any individual in the course of his life fulfils a series of different kinship roles. Though their implications often need drawing out further, some aspects of this comparative anthropological research can be seen to be relevant to basic problems in family structure and family adjustment in modern industrial society.

The formal analysis of kin term systems, a classical theme in social anthropology, has taken on added refinements in recent years. Internationally, controversy developed over the pre-eminence to be assigned to 'descent theory' or to 'alliance theory' in the interpretation of transfers of women and goods at marriage and in subsequent social relations between members of different kin groups. The various conceptual schemes involved tended to assume either the primacy of lineage co-operation and the secondary role of marital unions, or the primacy of marriage as a necessary condition of social intercourse, and the secondary role of descent groups as aligned in ways which gave expression to this fundamental principle. In this controversy British anthropologists have been among the leading figures. Some of the forms which the argument took drew from a friendly American critic, Schneider, a commentary entitled *Some Muddles in the Models: or How the System Really Works*. Apart from clarifying the question of the use of such typologies in problem-solving, he drew attention to various significant issues which had emerged in the debate as needing further study—the structural role of marriage in segmentary systems; the notion of filiation; the ideas of graded strength of corporateness in exercise of group rights. These are all issues central to the understanding of how many forms of society still operate their status systems and control of wealth.

A special area of interest explored deeply by British social anthropologists in recent years is the structure and operations of caste systems. Here problems of kinship organization in relation to social stratification are most strongly emphasized.

15

Such studies not only throw light on a phenomenon which is still of pivotal importance in the life of India's villagers; they also contribute to the theory of the structural role of sectors in a total organic social system. Such caste studies have also had implications for the understanding of political and economic problems over wide areas of Asian society.

Parallel to research in such fields has been the investigation of kinship systems which lack the neatly defined descent-group arrangements characteristic of lineage alignment such as held the attention of British anthropologists for so long. Study of 'bilateral', 'cognatic' systems—sometimes despairingly termed 'non-unilineal'—has assumed increasing importance in recent years. Interest in the broad theoretical problems has reinforced a tendency of research in Britain and other Western countries to examine kinship patterns in industrial society. In addition to analysis of extended family relationships, kin networks, and kin terminologies, studies have also been made of the support which individuals and families receive from kin outside the family circle, on occasions of crisis such as pregnancy and confinement, mental illness or bereavement. Such investigations have practical interest for social policy as well as theoretical significance. Related studies based on the same general framework of kinship in London and Chicago point to interesting possibilities of development of trans-atlantic co-operation in such social science activities.

Other recent trends in kinship research have been in the direction of attaching greater importance to the significance for social action of individual commitments. The extent to which an individual's commitment to a given social pattern or system of social relationships is conditioned by his status interest, his property interest, his interest in his personal security and that of his family expresses itself to a high degree through his behaviour in regard to his kinship obligations. Studying the social effects of choice and decision in such spheres is very relevant also in understanding the processes of social change. This way of looking at the data, in terms of individual reactions to the notion of commitment, has been most fruitful where some empirical tests can be applied, as by money payments, transfers of women in marriage, or voting behaviour.

Political anthropology

If kinship study is admittedly a prerogative of anthropologists, this is not so with political and economic studies. Yet there is an anthropological contribution to be made to both. Intensive field studies undertaken in Africa in the 'thirties, which drew support from a growing public concern with problems of future development, provided a major stimulation to theoretical advances in political anthropology. These laid foundations for research and analysis into modes of political action and processes of social control which are still major fields of interest.

The study of politics by British social anthropologists is primarily concerned with relating politics as a sub-system (of ideas, of actions or both) to other social sub-systems. This concern for the social matrix for political action—the study of infrastructures both at the level of ideology and at the level of action—is not restricted to social anthropologists alone. It is shared by sociologists and has been part of the canon of political scientists since Montesquieu, if not always observed by them. But social anthropologists are usually much more conscious of the social context of political structures and political behaviour. Where the contribution of social anthropology to the study of politics is most marked is in its focus on micro-systems, on politics at the village level. (This micro-analysis by anthropologists can serve as very useful 'model-building' for political scientists.) But anthropological

17

studies of the macro-systems of the state and its institutions have been increasing in recent years.

The dominant method of anthropological analysis outlined a generation ago by Fortes and Evans-Pritchard is to seek for functional connections between political and non-political roles and institutions, to show how they support one another, and how deviance and crisis are controlled. In general more attention is paid to continuity than to change; search is made, so to say, for the 'eternal verities' of political action. It is this outlook which gives shape to general surveys of the contributions of social anthropology to the understanding of politics published in recent years, such as those by Mair and Gluckman. Classifying 'simple' political systems, conceived of as functional wholes, and study of the working and co-ordination of indigenous political institutions, continues to occupy a number of scholars. Programmes for comparative research in this field suggest the need for more systematically collected data; they also indicate that much theoretical work on the construction of typologies of simple political systems still remains to be done, and that effective comparative work is possible only within strict limits.

But the majority of research workers in the political field have been concerned less with typologies and comparison than with discovering how particular sets of institutions work, especially in coping with recurrent crises. There has been a strong interest in succession disputes, in measures for grappling with environmental disasters such as famine, in the stabilizing of apparently disruptive activities such as ritual defiance. There has also been a recognition, especially among anthropologists studying African politics, that the attainment of historical depth should be a major objective, in order to illustrate the special conditions and processes which have affected the structure and organization of the political system. Intensive studies of the political development of African societies during the period preceding colonial rule have provided material for the analysis of indigenous political processes. Some interesting studies have recently been made of clientship as a principle of political importance. But notably lacking so far have been studies of the routine processes of competition in politics. All such studies have concerned themselves with the categories through which the people of a given society have themselves conceived of their own activities; a few studies have addressed themselves directly to this question of indigenous 'political philosophies'.

The characteristics of this approach to the study of politics are: abstraction to a fairly high level, at least to a point at which a unified political system can be discerned; a consequent preoccupation with the normative rules of political behaviour rather than its pragmatic regularities; and a level of discourse which transcends the complexities and untidiness of plural societies and changing situations. This approach has brought to light the immense variety of 'primitive' political systems, the existence of 'acephalous' systems lacking not only a centralized authority but even recognized chiefs or other political leaders; and the considerable sophistication of some allegedly 'primitive' politics. It possibly speaks more directly to theory in other social sciences than does more 'engaged' research.

A weakness of those analyses which have seen the political sub-system as a part of a single functional whole is that they have tended to under-emphasize struggles between men and conflicts between rules. Conflict, instability and disorder are not, of course, disregarded, but the analysis has tended to be taken up only at the point at which some customary rule can be invoked to terminate the disorder. Yet political activity is essentially competitive, and short of the point at which some controlling institution calls a halt to the competition there is a richness of tactical and logistic rules which regulate the behaviour of the competitors. Sometimes referred to as 'social organization', this is best perceived by considering the actors not to be so many faceless automata, moving to and fro at the behest of structural rules, but as manipulators choosing within a range of possible tactics and asking themselves not only what they *ought* to do, but also what they *can* do. Various studies of significance have been made of what political entrepreneurs can do with and within the rules of political behaviour.

The analysis of politics as a set of tactical choices open to competitors in an arena, and the consequence of these choices, is not a radical departure from the earlier normative analyses of political structures. Rather it is an effort to make a more detailed analysis of the process of competition, taking into account a larger number of variables, especially logistic variables. Some stimulation has come from games theory, but the high degree of abstraction and the sophisticated mathematics required by that theory will probably prevent its extensive substantive use in social anthropology. Nevertheless, the entrepreneurial combinations of resources which political actors make in competition with one another look like becoming an important field of exploration in the coming years. This trend, which is in effect a development out of the dominant structural-functional analysis, forms a link with a second main category of political anthropology: the study of 'encapsulated' political systems.

At an earlier period most societies described in political terms by social anthropologists were encapsulated within a colonial administration. But this fact was noticed rather than built into the central analysis. Fieldwork in more developed peasant societies, in which a central problem is the connection between local communities and urban or administrative centres, and research in countries like India where the imperial regime and its predecessors have encapsulated village politics for centuries, made it quite impossible to envisage the local community as a whole, complete in itself.

This generated a number of problems: how the 'encapsulated' political system reacts to influences outside; how external institutions are transformed when they reach into the local community; and how the discontinuity between local and national or state levels is both maintained and at the same time bridged by some kind of communication. This category is especially rich in the description of roles and institutions which either by design or otherwise bridge the gap between the centre and the local polity, and of the normative conflicts which such roles usually involve.

Much anthropological work has now been done in situations where village politics are vitally affected by national politics. But it has raised a number of problems. The individual manipulator is in no danger of being lost behind the wall of structural rules: there is no such *one* wall, but rather a series of half-built or broken-down walls from which the political entrepreneur may pick and select his building blocks. Nor can the struggles which arise over innovative action be disguised as deviance, for what is deviant in one structure is right conduct in another. Interest in factions is also an interest in political innovation: a politician can be envisaged as selecting pieces of different structures to put together his new group of supporters. These situations invite the analysis of politics as a set of rules for making tactical choices. But we have yet to decide in large measure what kind of theory will help construct such models.

There also seems to be a problem of where to draw the line, for the interwoven causal connections between local polity and the encapsulating polity do not provide the apparently sharp boundary of a whole isolated structure. The use of such concepts as 'network' to some extent by-passes the problem of drawing boundaries around systems.

Probably the most important result of dealing with part-polities and with a multiplicity of political structures in one situation or field is that the social anthropologist must modify his earlier functionalist approach. We still try to connect sub-systems, but these sub-systems are not always consistent with one another; we are forced to consider causal relationships. If one role or institution waxes, then another must wane: in other words, an examination of encapsulated political systems cannot be adequately done without considering change. Here much of the work is still descriptive and particular: comparative generalizations have yet to be made.

The characteristic change in 'encapsulated' political systems is towards greater specialization of political role. When this happens, it pays less to explain political roles by setting them against the context of other non-political roles in the local structure and more to see them in relation to wider political institutions. But as political roles become more differentiated, do we then withdraw to make room for the political scientist?

Just as ethnographers still worry because the 'tribes' are vanishing, we are also faced with a loss of subject matter, inasmuch as political roles become progressively differentiated from other social roles? What should be the role of the political anthropologist, and what should be his relationship to the political scientist in the study of 'modern' societies, both our own complex society and the emerging nations of Afro-Asia and elsewhere? What are anthropologists, as distinct from political scientists, best fitted to do, if we set out to study political parties, local elections or local government in India, or parish-pump politics in Wales, Italy or Malta?

Our first asset is the technique of fieldwork, the long and intense effort to 'get inside' a relatively small universe of people. Modern political structures have official ideologies of great sophistication—objects of study in themselves. These ideologies lay down ends, policies, and tactics, and are based upon an explicit, if often mythical, statement of the national and international situation. But behind the official cognitive map of means, ends, and existential statements, lies a variety of other cultural maps, nearer to the level of action and showing features which do not appear on the official map. This is not only true of the 'grass-roots' level of politics: it can also be done for any fairly discrete group or even class, and is likely to be especially profitable in the study of élites, not least in the developing nations. This is, of course, nothing new for the anthropologist, because in the last resort the investigation seeks to find the relationship between 'official' political ideologies and local or traditional values.

Our second asset is experience in carrying out the analogous investigation in terms of social relationships. Although the trend is usually towards greater differentiation of political roles, even in the most 'modern' society these roles are never entirely differentiated, and all politicians operate through informal communication networks based variously upon caste, or kinship, or regional, or tribal, educational or class affiliations. (A few political scientists have also worked at this level in the developing nations, and co-operative research might be fruitful.)

An outline of what should be done in the field of political anthropology would include three types of research.

(a) Working out typologies of political systems in more refined developmental form, probably making increasing use of historical material and so building slender bridges, such as those which already exist between studies of cognitive systems by anthropologists, philosophers and historians.

(b) Within this field there is certainly room for more work on the 'tactical' processes of political competition, drawing inspiration from games theory, studies of conflict resolution, and various kinds of models.

(c) In the study of 'encapsulated' (i.e. only partly sovereign) political systems, which involve problems of change and progressive differentiation of political roles, an immediate need is for comparative summaries and general theory.[1]

Social control

Recently published studies by both anthropologists and lawyers on sociological aspects of indigenous legal systems have shown a convergence of interest between social anthropologists and legal scholars concerning the present and future position of indigenous legal principles and procedures. (The results of anthropological studies have notably influenced the views of such legal writers as Elias and Coker on Nigeria.)

A number of types of problem fall into the field of social control, or law in its broad sense. Every set of social relationships contains its own sanctions for default and breach of obligations. These sanctions include withdrawal of interaction, ridicule, reprimand, breaking of a chain of reciprocity, as against intensity of interaction, praise, reward, and re-emphasis of reciprocity. Nadel named the negative sanctions 'intrinsic penalties'. Since intrinsic penalties and rewards reside in the social relationships themselves, or in institutional milieux, this field of study has been very well covered by socio-anthropological research among tribal peoples. Studies of legal, moral, and ritual sanctions and their interactions indicate how social behaviour is regulated and the degree of nonconformity to rule. Comparative studies also draw attention to certain general principles. In tribal societies, situations involving conflict of principles are often handled by ritual and mystical beliefs, procedures, and actions: comparable proceedings sometimes ensue in our secularly oriented society.

---

[1] Among the publications in the list on p. 106 that deal with political anthropology are nos. 4, 10, 14, 23, 33, 35, 39, 48, 51, 58 and 67.

There is also a considerable body of anthropological work on sanctions in urban industrial society, particularly in the kinds of social controls found in firms and other organizations, and in different types of families and sets of kinsfolk. But much more work is required on the controls involved in educational institutions and voluntary associations. These are especially suitable subjects for research by social anthropologists, since only through direct, detailed observation of sets of interaction can intrinsic penalties be uncovered.

Tribal societies, by the variety of their systems of authority and types of social pressure, ostensibly offer us the greatest range of types of settlement procedure. We can find in these societies possibilities of comparing how authoritative judges operate, in courts which are, in some respects, akin to our own. Despite the few good studies of this kind of situation, much more research remains to be done; with the even more radical alteration of the structure of traditional courts, it is urgent that this research be done where it is still possible. In many of the developing countries these traditional courts are being replaced by courts of the central government, to a greater extent than under the former policy of indirect rule. Hence the newly established courts require study as they develop their embryonic procedures and powers. Any court operates through conventions which make it possible to operate statutory procedures and rules; and we now have an unusual opportunity to observe the development of such conventions, where the 'alien' magistrate is of the same wide ethnic group as the subjects of the court, but may be cut off from them by education and culture. In some territories we shall be able to examine how, for instance, African magistrates, with relatively little legal training, operate in tribes different from their own, with all the problems of both lack of knowledge of language (with the increasing importance of interpreters) and lack of knowledge of local customs and standards (with dependence on assessors). Here too we shall have an opportunity to study

25

the establishment and development of law schools,[1] and to examine what influence they have on the creation of coherent bodies of law and practice. Such schools were not necessary in traditional systems, since it was open for anyone to participate in court proceedings, and thus to learn how to administer the law. It is particularly important to examine how far schools of law, and the role of academics in law, operate in this situation of conflict of laws, particularly if the aim of legislation is to reduce the importance of individuals carrying their personal law with them. Further, we can observe what kinds of mechanisms for handling disputes develop if the new courts do not appear, to the people subject to them, to deal with the critical problems that they face. The influence of arbitrators and councillors may increase, and *sub-rosa* traditional authorities may continue to be consulted. The range of contexts, from the communities basically still involved in subsistence production to those in areas of differentiated and specialized activities, should give us insight into the development of law in general.

Arbitrators operating in the shadow of new developments will also be a focus of future research. It may already be too late for us to investigate the roles of champions-at-law, intermediaries, negotiators, mediators, conciliators and arbitrators in traditional systems; but wherever it can be done this is work of the greatest importance. Some good studies of these kinds of procedures already exist, but do not always present detailed enough records of the total process of dispute and settlement to be used in general comparative analysis.

In Britain itself, it should be emphasized, there is a great dearth of studies of the actual process of administration of

---

[1] A recent seminar on Concepts in African Law, in which law officers and legal scholars as well as anthropologists took part, achieved a notable consensus as to the need for sociologically oriented field research, and also for the incorporation of teaching on African social institutions in the law schools of African universities.

law, as against studies of the rules of law and judgements on specific cases. (The dearth is even greater than in the USA.) Little detailed work has been done on sentencing in various courts; and we urgently need studies of at least lower-level courts, in order to examine how different values and standards of magistrates, police, and lawyers, as against delinquents and litigants, influence the settlement of disputes. There has of course been much work on delinquents themselves, and some on the police; but we do not have studies to compare with those in the United States on judges and magistrates. There have been very few competent studies of the working of the jury system, though many discussions of its theoretical advantages and disadvantages have taken place.

The tradition of social anthropology has concentrated attention on the political processes involved in the enforcement of obligations and of redress for injuries. Research on the judicial process—e.g. the relation between the role of rules and of social power—has been less adequately handled, particularly for tribes without instituted courts. Major problems in theoretical jurisprudence are involved here: indeed, the very existence of law has been called in question by some authorities. Hence it is most important for comparative sociological jurisprudence that research in this field be encouraged. The task of assessing the extent to which standard rules influence processes of trial and judgement is most difficult; and the greater the variety of situations and systems from which we get data, the better we shall be able to develop our understanding of this critical problem. It involves careful evaluation of the social power of the parties and the judges or arbitrators; an examination of the nature of disputes based on thorough acquaintance with the position of the parties and current norms and standards; and a detailed recording of the process of trial, of examination and cross-examination, and of judgement. This involves looking at the technical rules of evidence, and how these are used to control the introduction

27

of facts. It should lead ultimately into an examination of such modes of reasoning as are involved in, e.g. analogies, which may lead us to the heart of the problem of how values, including changing values, influence the application of rules, as stated by codes or informants, in real situations of dispute. The importance of these studies leads beyond the narrow field of law itself to the use of language, as in the handling of social relations, in the furthering and concealing of social and individual interests, etc. Social anthropologists have done much work in the detailed explication of what is contained in such concepts, but more has still to be done in the legal field. (In Britain itself there is scope for detailed investigation of the relation between trial, evidence and judgement in courts.)

As students of society we assume that the referents and contents of legal ideas are related to social and economic conditions, and that the concepts—or at least their referents—will alter as those conditions alter. On the other hand, there is often some lag of legal conceptions and doctrines behind changing economic and political relationships. Studies in tribal societies have given material about the ideas of legal personality, contract, injury, responsibility, and debt. But much more work needs to be done in this field, and careful observations made of how ideas involved in these concepts change with new developments in the differentiation and fragmentation of relationships through increase in commerce. These analyses should focus on case material, to see how far specific doctrines and conceptions in tribal law are able to cope with newly developing situations and relationships: how far they develop or become obsolete, and what social difficulties ensue.[1]

Economic anthropology.
Economic anthropology is a sub-discipline of social anthropology, with a long history (for example, B. K. Malinowski's

[1] Among the publications in the list on p. 106 that deal with law and social control are nos. 17, 21, 35, 40, 47 and 50.

Argonauts of the Western Pacific, published in 1922, is a classic study of trade). But it has not until recently interested most British social anthropologists as much as have studies of general social structure and political systems. The term itself is relatively new, and there are many different interpretations of the extent to which analysis of economic behaviour in small-scale economies can effectively use the concepts, methods, and techniques of modern economics. One view maintains that the economist cannot help the economic anthropologist, since the phenomena in which each deals differ in basic premises. Rationality, it is argued, differs in primitive and advanced economies, and different laws of supply and demand apply; non-monetary economies are basically different from monetary ones. Another school of thought maintains that while economic *institutions* differ widely, economic *concepts* and *principles*, as developed in complex societies, in general apply also to small-scale economies. The implication from this is that the economic anthropologist should be conversant with economic theory if he is to interpret competently the phenomena he is studying. On this latter view, which seems to have growing weight, economic anthropology may help to give a more explicit universality to economic concepts by allowing these to be reworked to cover all types of societies, not only industrial societies. Economic history of countries in pre-industrial and early industrial phases offers much comparative data for contemporary economic anthropology. Conversely, anthropological reports provide primary records for future study by historians of fast-changing underdeveloped countries, including transitions from non-monetary to monetary economy. Most workers in this field also believe that economic anthropology has distinct value in the analysis of institutions related to economic growth (see pp. 31, 32, 58, 59). It is however generally agreed that economic anthropologists must also be trained as general social anthropologists, since the study of their subject matter involves an understanding of the overall social structure of the society they are investigating and of the systems of beliefs involved in its moral, ritual, and religious systems.

The major focus in economic anthropology is on the comparative study of small-scale economic systems, ranging from those of isolated, technologically primitive communities to those of peasants strongly influenced by industrialization. (Economic systems of the industrial societies themselves have so far in general been excluded, although scope has been found for the application of economic anthropology to under-developed regions of industrial societies—e.g. crofter and cottage economies in the British Isles.) The field covered includes: land tenure; methods and organization of production; mobilization of a labour force and division of labour; occupational mobility; entrepreneurship; spheres and circuits of exchange; market institutions; forms of money and credit; levels of consumption and standards of living; the distribution of wealth in relation to social status. Theoretical studies in economic anthropology are still relatively few, though several general textbooks now being written may be expected to bring together points of current conceptual interest. What comparative work there is tends to contrast different forms of livelihood within the same culture and area, for example traders and non-traders; economic behaviour of dry rice and wet rice cultivators.

Many British contributions to economic anthropology have been concerned with the economics of cultivation, the effect of land reforms, the growth of farms and cash-cropping, labour migration, and the relationship between landholding and other aspects of the social structure. Studies of types of production in hunting and gathering and pastoralist societies have been made, but in terms of relationship between ecology, means of subsistence and general social structure rather than of economic anthropology as such. However, some work in economic anthropology has been done on fishing (cash trade) and on early developments in specialization and production of non-food items for trade. A good deal of recent work has been done by British anthropologists on spheres of exchange; markets and their operation; credit and interest; and the operation of indigenous money. Recent work has also included studies of saving, and the use made of capital in raising future consumption levels. Since today only dwindling enclaves among the populations of the world have remained virtually isolated from an external commercial market, studies of the effects of wage labour, commercial crop production, and external trading on the restructuring of social relations and groupings in African, Asian and Oceanic communities have increasingly engaged the attention of anthropologists over recent years.

All these topics may have some implications, positive or negative, for economic growth. Studies specifically concerned with economic development have in particular taken up investment and enterpreneurship; for example, anthropologists and an economist have collaborated in a series of essays on the accumulation and use of peasant capital. Barriers to economic growth have been emphasized in discussion of 'traditionalism' in indigenous systems.

Economic anthropology is potentially one of the most important branches of anthropology. This can be partly documented by its extraordinarily rapid development in the USA over the past five years. Although some of the best pioneer studies were done by British social anthropologists, or social anthropologists working in Britain, leadership in this field (in terms of number of anthropologists and number of studies) is tending to move to the USA.

Certain theoretical aspects of economic anthropology need particular attention by British scholars at present: social factors in economic growth; small-scale economies as systems (games theory, quasi-mathematical models); trade and exchange (operation of markets; spheres of exchange); exploration of some economic concepts (e.g. supply curves for labour) in the context of small-scale societies. Discussion of these topics is becoming more sharply focused and suggests that at this stage some more work on them will lead to a consolidation of knowledge. It is advantageous to support such growing points.

The continuing expansion of studies of development and growth as part of economics will continue to stimulate economic anthropology, and the growing gap between rich and poor nations, as well as the administration of aid programmes, are practical problems of great magnitude to which research in economic anthropology can contribute.

Here the relationship between economic anthropology and other discipline points to the need for interdisciplinary research. Participation of British social anthropologists in international conferences (e.g. on economic development in subsistence and peasant agriculture; on social prerequisites to economic growth—UNESCO/SS/38, 1964) has shown the possibilities of working on both the theoretical and practical aspects of such common problems with economists, political scientists, sociologists, and historians. For such collaboration to be effective it is necessary for the economic anthropologist to have a thorough knowledge of the relevant economics— not to a level at which he can make professional contributions to economics, but to a level at which he can ask meaningful economic questions and understand economic contributions to his field. (It would also be preferable for the economist to know some anthropology.) One necessity here is for more work to be done on codification and analysis of existing material in both fields and assessment of its significance for economic anthropology. Without this aid, economic anthropology will develop more haphazardly, with wasteful repetitions and without standard methods of approach. Fundamental enquiries of this type need at least as much support as field research of the sort that will result in descriptive monographs, valuable though the latter are in widening our knowledge of types of economy.[1]

Ritual, religion and cognitive systems

In the latter half of the nineteenth century, when the study of exotic cultures first began to acquire academic respectability, descriptions of 'primitive superstitions' and 'savage rites' constituted a very large proportion of all ethnographic literature. The basic doctrine of the social evolutionists was that at any particular stage of social development all men were of similar psychological disposition. This fact, it was supposed, could be most easily demonstrated in the case of beliefs about metaphysical phenomena and attitudes to problems of cognition. Indeed, down to about 1922 the influence of anthropologists upon thinkers in other academic fields came almost exclusively from their discussions of magic and the attributes of primitive thought. The works through which this influence was achieved (e.g. those of Tylor, Frazer, Lévy-Bruhl) treated the general field of metaphysical belief as something quite separable from that of economic action. In contrast, the central thesis of Malinowski's work was that social behaviour is an integral whole. So, he argued, we cannot hope to understand the nature and significance of 'magic' until we have examined it against its overall social and economic context. Functionalism in this sense thus tended to alter the anthropologist's priorities. In recent years social anthropologists have usually written about primitive religion not as a means of exemplifying primitive mentality but as a frame of reference through which one may observe a particular social system viewed as a whole. Religion is commonly

---

[1] Among the publications in the list on p. 106 that deal with economic anthropology are nos. 8, 19, 25, 29 and 41.

33

regarded as a means to or guarantee of material welfare. Likewise the specialist studies of Melanesian 'Cargo Cults', of which there has lately been a fair number, pay quite as much attention to background features of political, economic, and social organization as they do to the subtleties of theology.

Some notable advances have recently been made in the study of ritual symbolism, with particular reference to the analysis of African cosmological doctrines and basic categories of thought. Detailed studies of conceptual categories as expressed in communal and healing rituals have revealed a complex range of symbolism with interlocking connotations. Oppositions between pairs of categories over a wide range of natural phenenma, cultural elements, and social relations have been shown to be built up into a conceptual scheme which is drawn upon for the symbolic expression of social norms and cultural values.

The semantics of statements of belief and of ritual acts has been explored in the different contexts of modes of livelihood and social relations. Explanatory concepts associated with ancestral cults, particularly with reference to doctrines concerning the sources and control of human personality, have also been the subject of recent studies.

But social anthropologists have usually devoted more attention to the operational consequences of metaphysical beliefs than to the logical structure of the beliefs themselves. Thus, most studies of African witchcraft and sorcery have sharpened our understanding of the way in which witchcraft beliefs can function in the arena of small-scale domestic politics, but they have not done much to clarify the psychological and philosophic issues involved. Indeed, the converse may be the case. As our ethnographic knowledge mounts up, 'commonsense' distinctions between the rational and the irrational become increasingly difficult to sustain. Many anthropologists now feel much *less* confident that they understand the basis of non-European cognitive systems than did their predecessors of the previous generation.[1]

Modern studies of witchcraft phenomena are only a special case of the rather widespread application of role theory to social anthropology. The main ideas here originated in the work of Van Gennep and of Max Weber early in this century. Nearly all social anthropologists now feel impelled to demonstrate in their field material the existence of a social *system* consisting of a set framework of 'offices' which stand in more or less permanent relationship one with another. In the course of his life cycle each individual passes through a series of such 'offices'; one major function of 'ritual' is to act as marker for such transitions and to define the role obligations of particular office-holders. Over the years the description and analysis of such 'rites of passage' has become increasingly sophisticated. One aspect of this work is that it demonstrates the difficulty of establishing any clear-cut distinction between 'religious ritual' and 'secular ceremonial'. These forms of behaviour may well serve, in similar as well as different ways, both communicative expressive ends or as a form of psychological catharsis.

Although fieldwork is still dominated by the Malinowskian functionalist tradition, it is already apparent that the theoretical writings of Lévi-Strauss are beginning to have a marked influence on kinds of fact which functionally orientated fieldworkers manage to observe. Lévi-Strauss's concern is with the characteristics of mankind as a whole rather than with the attributes of any one functioning cultural system. He is interested in such very general problems as the nature

---

[1] Whatever style of analysis be adopted, it is always the case that 'ritual' materials present the investigator with problems of extraordinary complexity. Consequently, one persistent feature of the anthropologist's study of religion is that there has often been an exceptionally long delay between the original research and the printed publication.

of the thinking process, and the way cultural information is organized, stored, and perpetuated; he is thus led to a functionalism of a new kind. Where Malinowski sought to show that metaphysical beliefs and non-rational ritual acts could be functionally 'useful' when viewed against the total cultural background, the implication of Lévi-Strauss's analysis is that the irrationalities of metaphysical systems result from inherent requirements of the thinking process as such.

One over-simple way of describing the difference between the functionalism of Malinowski and the functionalism of Lévi-Strauss is to say that whereas the former was concerned to show how apparently irrational acts, observed in their context, could be seen to serve a *rational function or end*, the latter is attempting to resolve the same kind of difficulty by showing that irrational acts function so as to *convey messages*. Malinowski was inclined to ask: 'What does this action *do* in its total context?' Lévi-Strauss asks: 'What does it *say*?' Lévi-Strauss, therefore, sees the task of the anthropologist as equivalent to that of a linguist trying to analyse the grammar of an unknown language, and many of the analytical procedures which he recommends for the analysis of ethnographic materials are borrowed more or less directly from the armoury of general structural linguistics.[1]

Understandably, such adaptions work best when the ethnographic material is itself of a verbal kind. Lévi-Strauss's own ingenious analyses of mythologies from North and South America have provoked imitations of all kinds. Apart from miscellaneous essays there are at least three symposia 'in the press' at the time of writing which are a more or less direct

---

[1] An influence which is parallel to that of Lévi-Strauss, and to some extent coincident with it, derives from Oxford, with translation into English of a number of germinal 'structuralist' essays by E. Durkheim, Mauss, and Hertz, which originally appeared in French around the beginning of the century.

response to Lévi-Strauss's proposition that myth and ritual form a 'language' of communication which is capable of being decoded. A good deal of this work consists of a re-examination of existing ethnographic publications—for example, a new look at Radcliffe-Brown's classical account of Andamanese mythology. It remains to be seen whether fieldwork conducted with this explicit orientation turns out to be significantly different in consequence.[1]

Such views have led social anthropologists engaged in field research to pay closer attention to the internal structure of systems of metaphysical ideas, as distinct from either the superficial content (which fascinated the early evolutionists) or the utilitarian function (which has been the central interest of the post-Malinowski generation). Research workers are no longer content to report the facts about exotic beliefs, they want to 'break the code'. In the now widespread interest in systems of primitive classification, rather surprisingly the work of American anthropologists such as Conklin, which seems to link up with this area of enquiry, has so far had little influence on British anthropologists. Nor have British anthropologists so far done very much to pursue one obviously very important line of enquiry—namely the 'logic' of ideas lying at the back of 'magical' healing rituals. There is, however, a growing interest in the study of symbolic systems, ranging from S. F. Nadel's general observations on symbolic behaviour to V. W. Turner's extremely concentrated analysis of a small set of Ndembu ritual symbols (66).

Orthodox functionalism insisted that the study of belief and ritual can only be usefully pursued when the observer pays profound attention to 'context'. But while such studies are

---

[1] So far the influence of Lévi-Strauss has appeared only in the way the material is finally presented in printed form. The consequences of reading Lévi-Strauss *before* going into the field have as yet barely begun to appear.

still valid, other types of study are also important. For some writers at least, primitive religions are again coming to be thought of as self-sufficient autonomous systems. This attitude may lead back in future research to the kind of intensive ethnographic observation which was characteristic of the best monographs in the pre-Malinowski era. It is a legitimate criticism of functionalist anthropology that authors were often so keen to show just how *all* ethnographic facts fitted together 'as social glue' that they were inclined to ignore details which seemed functionally irrelevant.

During the past few years British anthropologists have shown a marked revival of interest in problems of classification, including the phenomena of 'totemism', taking that concept in its broadest possible sense. The basic question here is: what universal principles, if any, govern the ways by which men come to classify the things in the world and the relations in society? The issues involved are enormously complicated but of very wide interest. They overlap with enquiries which are currently being pursued in a variety of other academic fields, both in the sciences and in the arts. On the science side, investigations into the mechanisms of visual perception, speech formation, and the processes of verbal utterance serve to link the anthropologist's interests in classification and category-formation with fundamental problems in experimental psychology and general linguistic theory. These same anthropological interests link up with those of the logician, who has for too long tended to assume that the grammatical structure of Indo-European languages is basic to all rational human thought. There is a feedback here into the most orthodox of all academic disciplines, that of classical philosophy and ancient history. A recent book about the pre-Socratic philosophers makes extensive use of the recent findings of anthropologists concerning primitive classifications. M. I. Finley, in a variety of publications, has been demonstrating that the anthropologists' recent analyses of myth contain much that is relevant for students of Homer. Thus the 'armchair anthropologist', who has been an object of contempt among classical scholars and fieldworking anthropologists alike for the past thirty years, may well be due for a comeback. No one would now want to write another *Golden Bough*, but the biblical and classical materials to which Frazer and Robertson Smith devoted their over-imaginative attention eighty years ago deserve to be looked at again in the light of later anthropological insights. Some work of this type is already in progress.

Until quite recently it has been taken for granted that the only proper field of *anthropological* investigation of religion is in 'primitive' society. This has meant, in practice, that the so-called higher religions (Christianity, Judaism, Islam, Buddhism, Hinduism) have been excluded from serious anthropological attention. The conventional argument has been that these religions are commonly encountered in contaminated form; the anthropologist can quite properly investigate the contaminations, but the pure theology itself is outside his province! In the case of Buddhism and Hinduism, at any rate, this kind of discrimination is now breaking down, and a number of workers have been showing how greatly our insights are advanced when the study of the higher religions is seen as a problem of sociology rather than of comparative ethics. Comparable objective analysis of Christianity still lies largely in the future, though some explicit attempts have been made to apply an anthropological style of analysis to materials which have ordinarily been treated as a strict preserve of theologians and biblical historians. Meanwhile, we require many more studies of the behaviour and ideas of congregations of worshippers in Western religions, analysed in their social context.

A rather similar consequence also flows naturally from the fact that the social anthropologist's field researches are no longer narrowly confined to 'primitive' societies as traditionally understood. Studies of the political role of the cult of saints in contemporary Malta and Morocco, and of Mediterranean value systems centring around the concepts of 'honour' and 'shame', derive from Christian and Moslem countries which in the fairly recent past would have been deemed to lie outside the anthropologist's province. Another unorthodox field of enquiry in which several prominent anthropologists are showing interest is the relationship between 'ritual' as ordinarily understood by the anthropologist and 'ritualization' as understood by the ethologist. Are there principles of 'non-verbal' communication which are manifested in the stereotyped behaviours of human beings as well as in the stereotyped behaviours of other animals? Here again research is only just beginning.

To sum up: much recent and current anthropological work in the general field of 'ritual and belief' is dominated by the now orthodox premises of Malinowski functionalism. It is assumed that the concern of the research worker is to observe behaviour in its social context, and to achieve understanding by relating behaviour to context. This work is specialist in nature and depends on extremely intensive field research. It generally implies scepticism about the value of grand-scale generalization and wide-ranging cross-cultural comparison. But such work, however meritorious, is necessarily of rather limited interest to workers in other disciplines. Alongside this continuing interest in specialized functionalist studies there has recently been a marked revival in work of a broader comparative kind, leading to generalizations about the nature of mankind as distinct from the function of particular ritual systems. Purists may object, but anthropologists have some qualification to attempt such generalizations. A major defect of the old style anthropological 'comparative method' as practised by Frazer and his contemporaries was that the sophisticated Western European was usually left out of consideration. The newer style comparative method assumes that the basic processes of thought are essentially the same in all kinds and conditions of men and that broad-scale comparison is one of the ways by which we can gain small insights into these fundamental human mental processes. The main contribution of British social anthropology in the immediate future is still likely to derive from specialized detailed research in single well-defined cultural situations, but the functionalist emphasis in such work may well come to be re-orientated so as to make it more amenable to cross-cultural generalization of a fundamental kind. The latent possibilities here are exciting.

Anthropological studies of developing societies
The areas traditionally studied by anthropologists have been undergoing rapid development, especially during the last twenty years. Such 'development' involves changes in the political, social, and economic order. It has been likened with some justification to the Industrial Revolution in Western Europe, and many of the problems are similar. They include for example the effects of technological innovations on social life; the introduction of a monetary economy into economies which have largely been subsistence-based; and settlement in industrialized areas where the rural migrants concerned have to adjust to urban conditions of life and labour. An added complication is that traditionally based authority structures may have to be reconciled with the 'rational' requirements of modern administration. The anthropologist's business is to make sense out of this apparent cultural clash and disorder. His task is the more difficult because, despite the emergence of new patterns of social behaviour, much of the older way of life still continues.

Many studies have been made by social anthropologists of the social effects of technological change in communities undergoing development. A classic case here is the change in the system of division of labour created when ploughing

41

by oxen was introduced in South African tribes who previously practised hoe cultivation. Agriculture was previously the work of women and care of cattle the work of men; the yoking of oxen to the plough led men to undertake the cultivation of the soil, and gave them rights over the crop which they had previously not possessed. Comparable examples are studies of the changes produced by the introduction of irrigation to areas previously farmed by dry-cultivation methods, in India, or of the replacement of sail-powered fishing boats by diesel engine-powered boats in the fishing industry of the north-east coast of Malaya. Results of such changes may include an increased gap between richer and poorer peasants, and a reduction of earning power in the more vulnerable economic categories, such as women or children or partially disabled. They may also facilitate a change from traditional modes of leadership by ascribed status to leadership on the basis of new skills, or new opportunity to demonstrate business capacity.

Studies of the economic and social effects of replacing systems of customary payments in kind by money payments have demonstrated the complex nature of the situation. For instance, in some societies money swiftly replaces traditional media of exchange; in other societies money is regarded as an appropriate medium of exchange in certain contexts, but not in others; ceremonial transactions still demand traditional media, such as shell armlets or cattle, which are bought for money. The introduction of money transactions, linked with provision of new markets for land, products, or labour, has meant a re-structuring of modes of production, increasing the advantages of some people and reducing those of others. On the whole, traditional authority has suffered, the bonds of kin-groups have been weakened, and more scope given to the satisfaction of individual interests as against group interests. Yet stimulus has been given to the emergence of new categories of entrepreneurs, with development of new patron-client relations. (It has been argued that in India, for example, a tendency to concentration of wealth in a few hands may be paradoxically a potential form of community saving; if the poor are forced to accept a low standard of living, the reduction in their consumption can become a source of investment. Yet economic advantage depends on how the savings are spent—an increase in total output of the economy by no means necessarily follows.)

Various studies have been made in India and elsewhere of the movement and adaptation of peasants to life in established cities. But much of the research in the field of urbanization has been conducted among labour migrants in 'new' mining and other industrialized towns of Africa. In sub-Saharan Africa these investigations have been concerned with the kinds of social alignments which result from the association of people of different tribes, including the interaction of 'urbanized' and 'rural' Africans. Tribalism in the Copperbelt, for example, involves a feeling of belonging to certain categories, these being defined on the basis of broad cultural differences. Tribalism in these terms does not connote corporate groups, but as a principle of association it facilitates harmonious relations between comparative strangers. Yet urban dwellers give allegiance and loyalty to tribal leaders in some situations and not in others. Ordinarily, Africans working on the Copperbelt have respect for their elders, but in a strike the elders lacked all influence because it was the workers' common interests as miners, irrespective of tribe, that prompted this industrial action. Prolonged residence in the atmosphere of the town does not automatically change country-bred Africans into townsmen. The individual person has a choice: certain relations, at work, are thrust upon him, but outside working hours he voluntarily decides upon his associates. To become urbanized the trivally-oriented individual must select new habits and also new companions and friends; he must be ready to accept in place of his people at home 'real' townsmen as his reference group. Here the playing of 'urban' and of 'rural' roles may alternate.

In Western Africa, the racial division of labour is less clear-cut and there is less discontinuity between rural and urban social behaviour. Seasonal migrations over short distances and the constant coming and going of traders tend to enfold neighbouring rural areas within the same social and economic system as that of the industrialized towns. Since 'development' in this case involves participation by Africans at every level of society, several investigators have treated the transformation of local structures as integral to a generalized urbanization process. Thus, in the case of kinship, with education and with the separation of the domestic group from the lineage, there is a tendency for the conjugal relationship to alter and for the ideal to become a marriage relationship of companions. Various investigators have stressed the wide variety in types of marriage and domesticity found nearly everywhere and the fact that the predominant pattern of family life continues to be influenced by tribal culture. In Kampala, for example, for most urban migrants inter-tribal marriage may be a passage from a temporary common law marriage to recognized permanent union, and permanence usually necessitates one of the partners 'becoming' a member of the other spouse's tribe. That indigenous beliefs are still influential in African towns has also been emphasized in studies of new witch-finding and syncretist cults. According to some data, the rituals of these groups serve to 'rationalize' worries and anxieties arising from urban life for which the traditional religion has no answer.

New forms of social stratification, including the position of élites, have been studied, especially in parts of Africa. The findings generally stress the importance of occupational and educational factors, and the fact that class consciousness is modified by loyalties to tribe or kin. As a result of kin sentiment the upward mobility of one individual can be followed by the upward mobility of a wide range of relatives; while structural opposition serves as one of the processes by which urban immigrants are absorbed in the urban system. Thus, in the case of Freetown in Sierra Leone, the resuscitation of tribal pride among the Temne led to the young men's companions performing an adaptive function. The contribution made by voluntary associations in general to the 'integration' of the heterogeneous populations of growing West African towns has been explained in large measure in such terms.

Anthropological studies of political change have often been concerned with the functions of traditional authority. An investigation has been made, for example, of differences in the adaptation made by 'statelike' and by 'stateless' types of political systems to modern local government introduced under British rule. Analysis of conditions among some Ugandan and Tanzanian tribes elucidated the difficulties of reconciling indigenous ideas of leadership with concepts of 'democratic' government. In the resulting compromise, the position of the chief appeared to be particularly ambiguous. Either he became a 'Government stooge' in the eyes of his followers, or was regarded as 'disloyal' or 'inefficient' by the administration. The appearance of political parties makes this kind of situation even more complex, and the traditional ruler may be torn between the interests of his community and those of the dominant political party.

The scope for further anthropological study in developing societies is very great indeed. In various Asian, African, and Oceanic societies political scientists have carried out a considerable amount of research on the central organs of government both before and after independence, for example, work on national assemblies; the composition and running of the new civil service; party organization and the effects of the electoral system. However, beneath the more modern trappings of government, traditional groupings and loyalties

45

persist; and it also seems to be the case that in the smaller towns and in rural areas most associational activity is controlled by a relatively small group of individuals. Some anthropological study of these 'grass-roots' of politics has been carried out in India, but much more research is needed elsewhere to elucidate the whole process of decision-making at a village and district level. These are the levels which seem to be of fundamental importance for the implementation of the many schemes of development, welfare, rural betterment and settlement which are now being financed.

Often related to the latter problem, particularly in African towns, for example, is the part played by voluntary associations in articulating old and new institutions with one another and with bureaucracy. Many urban migrants become members, but we need to know more precisely which migrants join and which do not, which joiners become activists, why migrants join some associations in preference to others, and what is the role of these new types of association. Further, if it is true that these organizations perform an 'adaptive function', research must now identify the conditions under which varying degrees and kinds of adaptation occur, the socio-cultural elements which are more or less amendable to adaptation, and the relative contribution which voluntary associations make to adaptations *vis-a-vis* other social structures. We also require more information about the emergences of élites. Some work has been done on this, for instance in Malaysia and in Africa. But there is need for the study of this phenomenon and its relationship with traditional society.

No less central to development in general is the question of family organization and function. Investigations made in Africa have pointed to the emergence of the domestic group as a socio-economic unit on its own, but both there and elsewhere research is needed to show more precisely the nature of the conjugal relationship, the effect upon the welfare and upbringing of children, and the conditions that conduce towards or inhibit stability in marriage. This problem is complicated by the prevalence of irregular unions, the incompatibility of monogamous marriage with traditional kinship norms, and the wide variety in marriage types. What is needed, therefore, is a series of studies made in different societies and at different levels of literacy and occupation. These investigations should employ a standardized procedure so that effective comparisons could be made of the factors affecting marriage type and family organization. Studies of religious groups, including the differential adaptation of Christians and Moslems to social change, would also be relevant in this connection.

There is need for long-term research in order to predict future trends in 'development' itself. The countries concerned have taken over much of the technology of the West and employed many of its institutions as models. It cannot be assumed, however, that further change will be uniformly in the same direction and of the same character. Many African countries, for instance, have adopted single-party government; and the growth of city life does not necessarily appear to be marked by the anonymity and individualism regarded as characteristic of Western urbanization. Doubtless in these regards the persistence of tradition is an important factor, but we require to know much more about the new mechanisms which have begun to operate and the kind of social and other circumstances in which the value systems and institutions concerned take shape.

Embryonic nationalism is a case in point. It could be studied very profitably in Oceania where, since many of the island territories are being prepared for independence, during the next decade there will still be the chance of observing the emergence of new nation-states from the very dawn of independence. It will not be necessary to commence investigation when self-government is already a *fait accompli*, as in other parts of the world. Comparative studies could be made between the New Hebrides, Papua and New Guinea, and the British Solomon Islands.

In the more industrialized countries of Africa the situation is different, because improvements in communication, wage, employment, etc., have already brought much of the rural area within the same economic system as the town, and in India the process has gone much further. In the developing countries India has by far the most sophisticated economy, the most efficient civil service, and the most developed organs for community development of any country in developing Africa and Asia. Furthermore, the effort at planned engineering and calculated change in social values and social structure is exemplified to a greater degree in India than in the African continent and in Oceania.

Since, therefore, many sociological issues turn on the extent of urban commitment rather than on rural/urban dichotomy, the more far-reaching requirements of research are likely to be somewhat similar to those of Western Europe. In other words, the anthropologist will need to study the social effects of population movement *between* as well as into towns; the implications of the developmental cycle of the family and of family size for housing; the factors which make for or mar 'community' stability, etc. It is likely also that he will be asked to throw light upon the problem of declining communities, both rural and urban; and to forecast the effects of transplanting industry in a rural setting. Analysis of these 'modern' problems is likely to bring the social anthropologist even closer to the sociologist, and in many cases it will involve an inter-disciplinary approach in which the services of political scientists and psychologists as well as other social scientists will also be required.

Anthropological studies of complex societies
Social anthropologists for long protested that their discipline was not confined to the study of 'primitive' societies, though

before the war very little research had been carried out in more advanced societies. Rapid developments after the war, a broader conceptual approach, and more opportunities for field research stimulated social anthropologists to study both rural communities and sectors of urban areas in 'civilized' societies. The range now covered is very wide—from Chinese agriculturalists, Malay fishermen, Indian caste groups to Maltese industrial labourers, Guyanese plantation hands, Greek shepherds, Welsh miners, Scottish crofters. Institutionally, studies have been made of kinship and neighbourhood relationships; factory relationships; friendship, patronage, and clientship; community leadership; voluntary associations such as youth groups, band clubs or religious sects; factions and alliances; social events such as funerals and Christmas reunions.

Entry into this field has posed some problems of scope and method for social anthropologists. Complex societies are marked by the extensiveness of the social relationships of their members, so that an adequate study of the social position of individuals in, say, a village community may demand a wide-ranging investigation into their economic, political, and recreational activities in a nearby town. Moreover, one important characteristic of complex societies is the number and distinct quality of role-relationships to be found therein. In a small-scale society of the kind traditionally studied by social anthropologists an individual interacts over and over again with the same individuals in virtually all social situations. In a large-scale complex society each individual has many separate roles which have an impersonal or part-relationship character; he interacts with many people in his social environment in one particular context apiece only. In a Malay village, a man buys fish from someone who is a neighbour, goes to the same mosque, and is probably connected by marriage; in an English town he buys fish from a fishmonger whom he probably never meets outside the shop. Complex societies are those in which roles tend to be more differentiated, more specialized, more 'universalistic' or impersonal—in Maine's terms, contractual relationships tend to replace status relationships. Hence the problem of definition of the field or unit of study continues to be a matter of some concern.

Research methods have tended to be modified to take account of these conditions. For instance, to take an extreme case—in rural community studies an anthropologist commonly accompanies a male informant to his place of work and discusses with him his technology in its social context; this is impossible if, as in one case in a study in London, the informant works in Buckingham Palace! Apart from access problems, knowledge of the social context usually demands much greater attention to documentary sources, and to the possibility of quantitative record, than in the conventional research by anthropologists in earlier periods. It is in such fields that the link between social anthropology and sociology becomes most evident.

But despite such new methodological demands, social anthropologists have been able to carve out for themselves areas of interest relatively untouched by other social scientists. In Britain the most evident of these has been the area of extra-familial kinship. Sociological studies of the family, on the applied side even more than on the theoretical side, have been carried out extensively in Britain for many years. But the significance of kin relations outside the nuclear family had gone relatively unperceived until research carried out or stimulated by anthropologists drew attention to the problems. The theoretical interest of such studies has been considerable in helping to throw light on forms of kinship typology hitherto not systematically studied, on kin rights and obligations, and on conflict among kin. In addition, such research into the full range of family and kin ties indicates an important field of investigation into factors involved in socialization of children, pregnancy and confinement, illegitimacy, old age, inheritance, physical and mental illness, and other social crises. Some significant evidence is also given of changing family size and the changing role of kinship ties in modern industrial society, especially in an urban milieu. Some data, still imperfect, are given on class differences in kinship patterns.

Another, though related, set of studies by social anthropologists is concerned with rural or small town communities in Britain, each aiming to exhibit the social structure and culture of the community concerned. Major emphases here apart from kinship have been on population movement and land tenure, community consciousness and cohesion, voluntary associations of a religious or recreational character, social status and stratification, local government and local politics. As in general anthropological research, the prime method of enquiry has been direct observational field research, often maintained as a participant in the community life.

Apart from community studies, anthropological research has also focused on the interpretation in more general social terms of the significance of well-known institutions of a professional or ceremonial character. Examples of this type of enquiry are investigations into: the social role of the police (11), and of advocates (barristers); the relevance of social class differences among university students; and funeral behaviour. Again, anthropological research among immigrants into Britain, or into minority groups among the general population, has been able to uncover a great deal of valuable data, previously not known, about their social structure, values, and patterns of living. To mention just one fact with possible implications for social policy, whereas English mothers have now been conditioned to feel guilty when they have their children placed in care by the local authority, it seems that many West Indian mothers with young children look upon this as an acceptable method of having the children well fed and clothed, and well educated. This relates to the different family structure in the West Indies, and illustrates how different social pressures may affect moral judgements of a mother's role.

Themes which have also been explored in some of these anthropological studies include the significance of geographical, occupational, and social mobility; the changing relations between the sexes, especially between husband and wife; the complexity of local status systems and social networks in long-standing communities; the problems of social living in new settlements such as housing estates.

Anthropological studies comparable to those in Britain have been made among complex societies abroad by British anthropologists. The Mediterranean is an area of special interest here, because of the ease of finding specialized local communities which can be studied by conventional anthropological techniques. The focus of attention in field location has usually been the nucleated village, of which the economy, family structure, social institutions, and value systems are analysed and interpreted. But attempt is normally made also to investigate relationships with the wider society and to estimate the effect of these on the community's internal relations. Problems arising from economic development, industrialization and urbanization have increasingly begun to claim attention. Studies have been made in Italy and Sicily of land tenure and land reform and their relation to local politics, of changing values among workers in a new industrial area; in Greece, of family structure in an industrial district of Athens; in Malta, of religion and politics in rural areas—published with the attractive and relevant title of *Saints and Fireworks* (14); in Yugoslavia, of the degree to which traditional kin ties affect modern agricultural development; in Spain, of the conflict between demands by the local community and by the central government. In all such studies the relation between the microcosm and the macrocosm, the small community and the great society, is posed and commented upon, as one of the crucial problems of the changing conditions of our time.

The direct contribution of British social anthropologists to studies of complex societies in other areas has necessarily been very moderate. Indirectly, however, their effect has been considerable, especially through the graduate training provided to nationals of Commonwealth countries in British departments of anthropology. This has been the case in Australia and New Zealand where a substantial proportion of research in social anthropology has been carried out by workers who received their graduate training in centres in Britain. Included in such research have been studies of the relations between rural and urban Maori in New Zealand, the adaptation of Maori to industrial life, and the social effects of miscegenation in New Zealand and in Australia. British training has been less pervasive in South Africa and in Canada, but in both countries has provided stimulus to research on the adaptation of indigenous peoples to economic development, urbanization and changing political conditions. Provision of British anthropologists to direct and conduct research in these fields still continues to some degree—a recent British study of the social structure and functioning of a longshoremans' (dockers') union in Newfoundland is an interesting example of industrial anthropology. But incentives to British anthropologists to undertake research in such Commonwealth countries (as distinct from emigrating to posts there) are lamentably few, though the problems of these complex societies are of great interest, both theoretical and applied.

Race relations

Race relations studies do not deal with a separate sub-division of facts within the fields of sociology and social anthropology. They entail the study of much of the data of both these disciplines, but from a point of view that concentrates upon

53

the interaction of groups. Though contact between groups whose members are outwardly distinguishable attracts maximum attention, from the social scientist's standpoint interaction between groups that are racially distinguished cannot be separated from other varieties of group interaction. The sociologist studying relations between white supervisors and coloured workers in a particular industry needs first to understand the implications of the supervisor-worker relationship, and then he asks what difference it makes if the parties are identified with different social groups outside the work situation. The psychologist studying the social distance expressed in respect of Negroes needs to compare it with that expressed towards persons of different religion or social class. From this two chief consequences follow: first, that the range of race relations studies is very wide, overlapping with many of the special fields of sociology and social anthropology; second, that much work done in these fields can also find a place in that of race relations.

In overseas territories British social anthropologists have in recent years conducted a variety of researches bearing upon the interaction of groups, but most of it has been conceived in terms of the study of cultural change or some other framework of ideas; this research has not benefited as it might from sociological and psychological studies specifically concerned with race relations.

With respect to race relations in Britain, the most striking feature has been the failure of research to increase in proportion either to the growth in racial tension and integration as a social problem, or to the great expansion in the number of teachers and students of sociology and social anthropology.[1]

---

[1] Of the 137 people who contributed details to the 1965 Register of Professional Sociologists in the UK, only 2 named race relations among their chief interests; of the 140 persons listed in the 1961 register of members of the Association of Social Anthropologists, 6 so mentioned it.

During the early 1950s a series of community studies in multi-racial localities was carried out by social anthropologists and sociologists, but though these studies left many gaps they have had hardly any successors. Some relevant information has been provided about Indian immigrants, but there has as yet been no general study of any Pakistani settlement and only one of a West Indian community. There have been some more specialist studies, for instance of West Indian pentecostal sects, and of housing and industrial absorption. But most of these remain single studies of particular localities; they need to be replicated to take allowance of local variation, of research workers' biases, and of contemporary changes. Fortunately, the declining interest within sociology has to some extent been balanced by the increased attention paid to aspects of the British racial scene by scholars in other disciplines, e.g. psychology, geography, economics, law, psychiatry, political science, and by a growing number of educationists.

Why should British social scientists in general, but sociologists in particular, not have shown more interest in studying race relations in Britain? The chief reason seems to be the way race relations is thought of as a social problem sphere, and is not seen as an area in which it is possible to carry out enquiries of theoretical interest to the general disciplines. The development of race relations studies in the USA has indicated the importance of a division of labour between the theoretical research of academics and the applied-science interest of the numerous agencies concerned to improve inter-group relations. Some of the agency staffs are primarily concerned to work out, for their groups, the implications of the findings of academic research people. This enables the latter to concentrate upon the studies that only they can carry through. With the growth of 'agency' work under the National Committee for Commonwealth Immigrants, Britain is moving out of the phase in which research work was identified with policy discussions and welfare activities. In this respect we are probably in advance of the Common Market countries which are faced with similar problems arising from labour migration.

The failure to see race relations studies as theoretically relevant to the disciplines has probably had a far more inhibiting effect than any shortage of research funds. This deficiency can be remedied only by demonstration, and a few general studies are at present in preparation which may have some influence in bringing together related material and stimulating thought. One example may be cited of the sort of gap to be bridged. A crucial issue in sociological theory concerns the relation between the collective interest of a group of people and their personal interests and actions as individuals. Situations of racial contact provide many instances where it is in the collective interest of the superior group to exercise restraint, but in the individual interest of members of that group to utilize their power in pursuit of personal gain. Again, there are instances where it is in the collective interest of the subordinated group to show solidarity but in the individual interest of members of that group to curry favour. Social theorists do not use the race relations literature on this and similar questions as they might, nor do students of race relations follow up sufficiently the theoretical implications of their material. A first priority should be to improve the interchange of ideas between theoretical discussion and empirical research in this field.

The study of race relations in Britain is in a rather special position in that university work is complemented by the activities of an independent body, the Institute of Race Relations. It has raised funds for the Survey of Race Relations, a five-year study due to conclude in 1968, which has in turn financed research. While the work of the Institute and the Survey may be of particular value in linking academic work to the interests of those concerned with the policy issues, there can be no substitute for the long-term, detached, thinking and analysis expected from university researchers. It is unfortunate, for example, that so little is being done in the universities to analyse integration as an ideal in terms of the kind of society into which immigrants are (presumably) to be integrated. Should it be assumed that the economy of the 1970s will make people more conscious of status differentiae? Should it be assumed that British people will continue to think that, other things being equal, a fair complexion is preferable to a dark one? If so, will the integration of second-generation coloured immigrants require their acceptance of British cultural values, including the one which stigmatizes them? Have the mass-media been able to re-modeel other disparaged attributes so that in local cultures they possess a certain dignity? There are major questions here about the nature of social relations in an industrial society.

Applied anthropology
Many of the findings of social anthropology can be seen to bear upon practical problems of economic development, improved government, and social welfare. But it is not a simple matter to define a sphere of applied social anthropology. While many anthropological problems can be seen to have practical implications, whether these are followed out depends upon how the problem is conceived and the context of the study. In the United States there is a society and a journal of applied anthropology, but in Britain there can hardly be said to be a sub-discipline of this separate character. Very few British social anthropologists have deliberately framed a research plan to solve a practical problem and conducted an investigation which could be termed applied anthropology from the start. But very many at some stage of their career have provided reports or given opinions on practical questions in connection with their work. These opinions have in many cases been concerned with analysis of complex social situations —epitomized in questions such as: why do these people refuse

57

to pay their taxes? why do those not sell their cattle when a good beef market is available? what is the reason for this land case or that succession dispute? Demonstration of the interests, loyalties, rights, obligations and values lying behind unco-operative behaviour has been more common than direct advice on how to change the situation. With the 'de-colonialization' of most of the territories in which social anthropologists have worked the pressures for the anthropologist to contribute in this way have lessened, and some of the consequent problems of adjustment of the anthropologist's role have disappeared.

But the field for applied anthropology is still wide, and many practical questions demand attention by social analysts who can isolate the most significant factors involved. Three fields may be taken for illustration.

Economic development
It is a matter of experience that many development projects have failed to reach their target because of poor communi-cation between planners and administrators on the one hand, and the people for whom the project is being implemented on the other. Study of the conceptual gap in such situations of mal-communication has been a theme of anthropology for many years. But there have been few investigations into the staff structure and channels of communication in development projects. No systematic typology of the 'command chain' has been worked out, nor have different types of structures been assessed for their effectiveness in widely different cultural situations.

A great amount of research by British social anthro-pologists has dealt with agriculture or pastoralism in some form, but most of the results are mainly of background value. With specific reference to agricultural development, British social anthropologist have carried out research on problems of adaptation of systems of land tenure to modern conditions. More follow-up studies, however, are needed to evaluate the effectiveness of measures introduced. Similar studies are required on the effects of new agricultural techniques, the working of agricultural co-operatives, and agricultural marketing arrangements. A parallel through more specialized field is the study of fishing communities, to which several social anthropologists have contributed. In the industrial sphere there have been many studies of the effects of labour migration, and anthropologists were the first to point out the radical effects on marriage and family life, and on the indigenous economic and political structure, of mass labour movements from rural areas to industrial employment. Most of this research has dealt with African conditions, and many more comparable studies are needed from Asian and other fields. Most earlier migration of labour was unplanned, but now that problems of labour mobility receive much systematic attention from governments and from employers, there is even more scope for continuing studies of the effects of the process on both the receiving and the home communities. Studies of labour relations in industrial enterprises, a field in which social anthropologists have already begun to make contributions, need to be considerably extended.

Medical anthropology

This is a very large and increasingly important field, to which a few social anthropologists have already made significant contributions. Theories of disease over a range of diverse cultures have been described by anthropologists interested in mind-body concepts, and studies of witchcraft and of spirit mediumship have shown the relevance of such beliefs to diagnosis and therapy. A few specific studies of the social context of illness have been made. The significance of this for problems of mental health, especially in conditions of rapid social change, has been demonstrated in various studies, for example in West Africa and in South Wales.

On the nutritional side some British anthropologists have

worked on social factors affecting diets in Malaya, New Guinea, and Central and East Africa. But economic development and urbanization bring changes in dietary habits, and there is great need for further studies in this field, especially since some nutritionists underrate the importance of social structure and values in affecting such food changes. It is not simply food taboos which need to be explained, but the whole set of relationships and conventions which dictate what foods are desirable and how they are prepared and apportioned.

In the sphere of sex relationships social anthropologists have been able to interpret and show the rationale of a range of exotic customs; and to explain the defensive attitudes of people to proposals to alter their traditional habits. A problem of cardinal importance, that of birth control, has engaged the attention of a few anthropologists. Despite the great technical progress in the development of contraceptives, and the propaganda efforts at their worldwide dispersion, deplorably little is known about the sexual attitudes and practices of the people in many of the societies affected. Mass attitude surveys, of which there have been a number, have been inadequate, and intensive anthropological research on factors affecting fertility, in which women research workers should play a most important part, is clearly required.

Other problems which require much more systematic attention by anthropologists include: the social background to indigenous medical practices; the social role of medical practitioners, and their relations with their patients and the community at large.

Education
Education of a modern type is apt to be the largest item in the budget of a developing country, yet its social components and implications have been almost entirely neglected by social anthropologists. Research could be carried out on many levels: the organization of the modern educational process

with relation to traditional forms (e.g. Koran schools, age associations); effects upon occupational structure and family life; education in relation to the career structure, social prestige, and marriage; the place of the school in the local community.

An example is the general problem of mass literacy. Much still needs to be found out about the social context in which the skills of reading and writing are most effectively learned. In the developing countries anthropological research could assist the educationist to design techniques more adapted to local situations. Anthropological research in the use of mass media and of visual aids can indicate difficulties which are apt to arise, and possibly lead to more effective methods of spreading knowledge at the village level. Again, study is needed on the type of education most appropriate to conditions of developing countries. Secondary school leavers often have difficulty in finding suitable employment, with consequent wastage of manpower. Information is needed on the process of transition from school to work—what sort of children are educated, how they find work, their subsequent careers, the changing position of girls through education, the extent to which they tend to compete with boys in employment after school—as well as on the comparative prestige attached to 'academic' type education and to 'vocational' education.

In the wider field a special problem is raised by health education. Every year a large number of health educators from developing countries are trained in Britain, as well as in other Western countries. Yet relatively little is known about the social background against which the health educator must work, nor about his role in the community, nor about the effectiveness of his activities in changing the behaviour of the people concerned. Studies already made by social anthropologists have shown the complexity and the difficulty of the problem, and the need for much further research. It is also clear that clarification of objectives is still necessary at the training level itself, and here it is urgently necessary to have the results of field research to feed back into the training situation.

The application of anthropological knowledge and techniques to problems of development and social change can not only be of assistance to the communities concerned and to technical experts and administrators involved in betterment programmes. It can also provide opportunity for interesting and significant field research. At a theoretical level, an applied anthropology project, properly set up, followed through and evaluated, can furnish a prepared setting for testing hypotheses. This means that the anthropologist should be consulted at the planning stage of the project, formulate his initial problem and hypotheses, make his predictions and recommendations on the basis of his field research, and then remain to follow through his enquiry to see how far these predictions have been borne out. An evaluation to show why they were or were not accurate should complete the study.

Three major difficulties enter into this situation. Most areas of research in applied anthropology require a special competence on the part of the fieldworker. He must not only be a well-trained social anthropologist; he must also be familiar with the basic framework of concepts relating to the particular problem area he is investigating. If the problem is one of changing a component in the diet of a people, he should have a working knowledge of the main principles of nutrition. If it concerns the introduction of a new crop he should know something about the agricultural aspects of the problem. In the past those anthropologists who have worked on such problems did usually accumulate a budget of the essential information required. But it is desirable for more effective co-operation with the technical workers concerned that he should receive some training in the discipline cognate to his problem. (In some cases, and most satisfactorily, the anthropologist has already received the appropriate medical, agricultural or other technical training.) This, however, may raise issues of timing and of financial support.

Another difficulty is of the reverse order. Experience has shown that it is often difficult for technical experts in a medical, agricultural or administrative field to see just where the contribution of the social scientist lies and just what conditions he needs for his research. For effective co-operation there must be a fair measure of agreement on the definition of the objectives of the research. This usually takes time to work out, and a willingness for each party to make adjustments in his conceptions of where the complexity of the problem under study lies.

A more serious difficulty in some ways is that of career structure. A medical man who takes up anthropological research, even if it bears directly on medical problems, runs the risk of getting out of line for advancement in his profession; an anthropologist who specializes in some field of applied anthropology has no clearly demarcated sphere of employment—in Britain at least—and is likely to be forced back into the ordinary academic market or take his chance in the wilderness of the international agencies. That an anthropologist who concentrates on problems in the applied field usually has some sense of commitment and moral obligation should not imply that his commitment should be its own reward. Those interested in the results of applied anthropology should direct attention to the need for securing the career conditions needed for the proper pursuit of such work.

3 Current Research Areas

Distribution

After the survey of anthropological research by major themes, the essentially comparative nature of social anthropology and its worldwide coverage can be brought out by examining the regional distribution of research interests of established workers. Information about areas in which they had conducted research at some time during approximately the last five years was supplied by ninety of the members of the Association of Social Anthropologists, including most of those resident in Britain. In round figures, 35 per cent of the area citations were to various parts of Africa, 20 per cent to areas in Asia, another 20 per cent to Europe, 15 per cent to areas in the Pacific (including Australia and New Zealand) and 10 per cent to America. That the largest proportion of citations referred to Africa is not surprising; it would probably have been greater fifteen or twenty years ago. What is interesting is the significant amount of work done in Europe, and the fact that within this, 10 per cent of the total research citations referred to work in the United Kingdom.

Africa and Asia

Only a brief mention can be given of the current position with regard to the scale and conditions of anthropological research in Africa (from British or Anglophone African institutions only). A rough estimation suggests that over the last few years there have, at any one time, been from fifteen to twenty-five British social anthropologists, mostly younger workers embarking on their first research projects, engaged in full-time field research in tropical Africa. Although the number of American social scientists recently working in Africa has been considerably greater, only a small proportion of these have had significant training in social anthropology and have been working primarily in that discipline. (American students of various aspects of the contemporary political scene, with a primary interest in problems of government, have out-numbered the social anthropologists.) The number of younger British scholars working as historians and mainly concerned with some aspects of political development during the colonial period in Africa has shown a marked increase over the last five years, and their studies have in some instances been initimately associated with related work in social anthropology, for example at the East African Institute of Social and Economic Research, and the Institutes of African Studies at the Universities of Ghana and Ibadan. The central agency for African research has been the International African Institute, whose headquarters are in London. Its first director was Professor Westermann of Germany, but for the last twenty-one years it has been directed by Professor Forde of University College, London, with the assistance of Consultative Directors (one African, two continental European, and one American) and an Executive Council composed of scholars from African and other countries. Through its journal *Africa*, the *Ethnographic Survey of Africa*, *African Abstracts*, and the many books it has published, as well as through research fellowships and an information service, the Institute has contributed directly to the development of British anthropology. Within an international framework it has kept British anthropologists in close touch with their African, American and continental European colleagues, and particularly in recent years has linked them with research institutions in Africa.

Africa is the region that provided a great deal of the field material with which much of the development of the theory of modern social anthropology in practically all its branches has been associated. There is still very great scope for anthro-pological research there, in a wide variety of types of changing social structure, from bands of nomadic hunters and gatherers to highly elaborate political communities.

In the Asian field the interest of British social anthropology has tended to be more recent. A substantial amount of research has been produced since the war from the Indian sub-continent. Not only in India and Pakistan, but also in Ceylon and in the Himalayan areas various research fields have been opened up as a result of British-based effort. Apart from investigations in 'tribal' societies, studies of economic development and social change have shown a special theoretical interest in changes in the caste system in modern conditions. The social and political significance of religious values (for instance Hindu attitudes to the cow) has offered a set of important contemporary problems, of which the fringe has as yet only been touched. A study of comparative forms of Indian traditional political systems in response to modern forces of change also awaits fuller investigation.

South-east Asia, Malaysia and Singapore provide examples of countries in which social anthropological research has been pioneered by British scholars, and in which British anthropology still has a considerable stake. Studies of Malay, Chinese, and Bornean social structure have prepared a framework for more detailed research, and given the first systematic accounts of the economic organization of family and marriage, and of a number of aspects of religion. Such work has indicated further research needs and, with British stimulus, significant studies, for example of rural credit, and of social stratification, are now being made by Malaysian anthropologists themselves. Thailand also is now becoming a centre for British anthropological research. The foothold so obtained in this part of the South-east Asiatic mainland opens on to a wide range of research fields, from highland tribal peoples to sophisticated townsmen.

Chinese studies are in a special category. Some of the earliest work in social anthropology in China came from British-trained Chinese scholars, and much of the best modern work on overseas Chinese social structure has been done under British auspices. Though Britain cannot match the scale of American effort in Chinese studies, the reputation of British scholars stands very high internationally. British social anthropologists are less interested than are the Americans in the study of China 'at a distance', but have focused primarily upon the Chinese in Singapore and Hong Kong. Here study of the basic modes and institutions of 'traditional' Chinese life is being supplemented by studies of modern change, including that in urban society. A novel effort in international co-operation and a focus for British research in this eastern Asian field is the London-Cornell Programme for Research in Far Eastern and South-east Asian Societies. Supported jointly by the (American) Carnegie Corporation and (British) Nuffield Foundation, this programme links relevant departments of the London School of Economics and Political Science, the School of Oriental and African Studies, and Cornell University, in research by anthropologists and other social scientists including economists and political scientists.

In Vietnam and Korea no British anthropological work has ever been done, although these countries share a common tradition with China. Japan too is almost a wilderness as far as research in social anthropology is concerned. British contacts with Japanese scholars are excellent, and a growing desire for British anthropological stimulus and participation in Japanese studies is evident.

Oceania and America

Oceania is another matter. There is some justification for regarding Oceania as the cradle of British social anthropology, but British-based research there has declined very greatly. This is a reflection not of lack of interest but of lack of support —British anthropologists are not infrequently recruited by non-British institutions for field research in Oceania. Melanesia is a classic region for the study of primitive art;

this is the pre-eminent area of 'cargo-cults'; the range of social structures in New Guinea is great; there has proved to be much scope for interdisciplinary research by anthropologists in collaboration with medical officers and agriculturalists. British scholars have contributed significantly in all these fields, but their work lacks continuity. Oceania generally and the Western Pacific in particular are a busy scene of international anthropological research, but for the most part British anthropologists are conspicious by their absence from it.

In some other areas of the world British effort in social anthropology has been small but not negligible. In Latin America investigation of some Indian communities has yielded data of great interest to kinship theory, while studies of peasantry are making contributions to economic anthropology. A programme of investigations in Latin America sponsored by the Institute of Race Relations in London has also enlisted the interest of some British anthropologists from the United States. In the Caribbean, the substantial earlier British contribution, largely through the Institute of Social and Economic Research of the University of the West Indies, has not been renewed, though a few studies from metropolitan Britain are still undertaken. This area has importance because it offers proven experience in the application of social anthropology to the study of complex literate societies in process of rapid change. A series of studies have been made on local systems of family and land tenure, plantation community problems, social stratification and mobility, and social and political aspects of pluralism. Such studies are also very relevant in linking up investigation of Caribbean conditions with the situation of immigrants from that region who have come to settle in Britain. The Research Unit for the Study of Multi-Racial Societies, established in the University of Sussex, has announced its interest in the Caribbean, and might well serve as a focus for British anthropological research there. With so many other countries also engaged there, however, it is of prime importance to establish international contacts in the planning and execution of projects.

Elsewhere on the American continent British social anthropologists have had special contacts with several Canadian universities and institutes, including one in Newfoundland, and Canadian training in social anthropology owes much to the British research tradition. There is much desire to have more British participation in Canadian research, and a wide range of problems for study. Yet the British commercial interest in opening up the Canadian northlands has not been paralleled by a comparable interest in the human populations, and the Scott Polar Research Institute at Cambridge does not have a social scientist of any discipline on its staff. It is argued that the greatest gap in the intellectual exchange in the social sciences between Canada and Britain lies in the absence of any single centre concerned with Canadian studies.[1]

EUROPE

Of all the regions, apart from Britain, that seem most capable of development for study, by British social anthropologists, Europe, especially Southern Europe and the Mediterranean, seems to offer most possibilities. British-based research has already produced substantial results here—from Turkey, Italy, Greece, Israel, Malta, Spain, Yugoslavia, Cyrenaica, Morocco (see text on complex societies, pp. 48–53). Four university departments or centres of anthropological study have already a declared interest in the region: Oxford, London School of Economics, Kent, Sussex. In addition to being easily accessible, relatively cheap in field costs and open to fairly close supervision of students, the Mediterranean

---

[1] It has been suggested that funds for such an enterprise might very well be forthcoming from Canadian financiers, who in general are interested in such international activities and concerned to promote good relations of the type such an institute might foster.

offers the prospect of ready co-operation with other social scientists. This has already been shown in the formation of a Committee for Mediterranean Studies by a combination of anthropologists, sociologists, economists and political scientists from the London School of Economics, the School of Oriental and African Studies, and the University of Kent. The Committee also includes consultant members from the University of Sussex and the University of Amsterdam. Provided with initial funds by the institutions concerned and by the Wenner-Gren Foundation for Anthropological Research, this Committee has already promoted research in social anthropology in Greece, Italy, Spain, and Algeria.

BRITAIN

Anthropologists have differing views as to their research role in complex industrialized countries. But the majority of British social anthropologists seem to favour a greater concentration than in the past on studies of British as well as of other European social institutions. Research by social anthropologists was begun in Britain at least twenty years ago, but has been of a very modest amount until recently. Sharing the field with sociologists might seem to create problems, but in fact the work to be done in description and analysis of social relations and social institutions in this country is so great that no real difficulties have arisen. Social anthropologists have tended to focus on special areas in keeping with their general interests—such as community studies, kinship, informal structures in working situations, race relations, religious cults. Where their work has overlapped with that of sociologists, co-operation rather than competition has resulted. Empirically, few anthropologists seem concerned with such demarcation problems. Some hold that field research in Britain or other industrialized countries should only come after research experience in a more traditionally 'exotic' region; others (who have tried it) point out that, under proper guidance, research into community relationships, or into genealogical structures and kinship ties, can well form part of anthropological training of students. There is, however, general agreement that while more research in Britain should be encouraged, this should not be stressed at the expense of field studies in other regions.

Field research into problems in one's own society presents special difficulties of *rapport*, and of gaining objectivity.[1] But it is important for comparative purposes, it offers relatively easy access and much less expense, and supervision of the research is much simpler. Moreover, there are many opportunities of making contributions to problems on which workers in other disciplines are also engaged. As work sponsored by the Medical Research Council and by the Tavistock Institute has already demonstrated, an anthropologist studying, for example, family and kin relations may co-operate effectively with a medical man or psychiatrist concerned with the social background to health problems. In view of the importance of this field, a systematic appraisal of research needs and possibilities in Britain over, say, the next five years is an idea that has commended itself to some anthropologists.

Regional priorities

Allocation of priorities between regions in anthropological field research is difficult.

Britain is a special case for development of anthropological field research in a much more systematic and problem-oriented way. Field research in Europe also offers the attraction of proximity and cheapness, as well as a range of complex social problems of both rural and urban kind.

---

[1] An interesting suggestion has been made that non-British anthropologists be sought to make studies of aspects of our society. This was in fact envisaged long ago, and one such study made by a Chinese anthropologist, but the results were not published in any systematic form. The experiment should be repeated.

A special point may be also made about British research interests abroad in dependent territories. There are certain sizeable territories in the world for which the UK government still has a specific direct responsibility, for example, Fiji, the Western Pacific High Commission, British Honduras, Hong Kong. It is a reasonable argument that the primary responsibility for obtaining systematic knowledge of the societies concerned and their reactions to modern economic and political changes rests with the British government. The only one of these territories which enjoys any substantial British research effort in social anthropology is Hong Kong, and this is not primarily by government effort. There is a clear case for much more social (including anthropological) research in these territories, where there is important material for theoretical development, and many practical problems demand urgent attention. In such research as is being carried out the British share is small, which gives the impression that these territories are neglected in this respect by the UK government.

But it can be argued that there is now a need to examine thoroughly the whole question of investment in anthropological field research on a regional basis, with a view to delimiting more precisely just which problems can benefit most from study, and where and for how long such study should take place, in the light of British resources available over, say, the next five years. Yet it is clear that this is not a unanimous view in the profession, and that it is widely felt that a fieldworker's selection of region for his research should be determined primarily by the nature of the problem and its relation to other problems rather than by any process of centralized decision.

Obviously research cannot be supported equally in all those regions in which British anthropologists have worked. But there are certain basic scientific needs to be satisfied. The comparative nature of social anthropology demands fresh supplies of data as new problems develop or classical problems are re-examined, and the vitality of theoretical research requires that a reasonable proportion of such data be collected in the field. From the training point of view too it is important for teachers to have had a range of different kinds of experience to draw upon. Regional or area research as such may be of little scientific interest. But each region offers its own unique set of scientific problems and field data, and among British anthropologists there should be some equipped for the study and interpretation of phenomena in each major region.

4 General Research Trends

Despite the vitality of social anthropology as a discipline, the present situation with regard to *field* research by professional social anthropologists is a somewhat static one. Indeed there are indications that there may be a falling off compared with the very rapid expansion of field research in the 'fifties. The very considerable body of research, including a number of major monographs, that has been published over the last five years (see the list on p. 106) is the outcome of intellectual and financial resources deployed in most cases a decade or more ago. Several underlying factors can be discerned so far as British work is concerned. First, the number of grants of the kind formerly provided by the Treasury Studentships in Foreign Languages and Cultures (Scarbrough Committee) and the Colonial Social Science Research Council has fallen away. Other grants now available are often subject to more limiting conditions. Second, the interest of American foundations, which generously assisted a number of British anthropologists at an earlier period, has now declined, partly because of normal periodic changes of programme, and partly because of more restrictive US governmental attitudes towards overseas academic aid. Third, the freedom enjoyed in their early days by the social research institutes established in Africa and the West Indies, both in the framing of projects and in the appointment of research workers, has tended to be restricted under changed conditions. The social research institutes have been incorporated in various ways in the organization of universities whose primary functions are understandably seen as centres for higher education and training to meet the urgent needs of the new states. The allocation of funds and administrative arrangements in connection with research programmes have sometimes been subject to delays. Save where it could be linked to some important aspect of higher education, such as study related to the pre-colonial history of major peoples, anthropological field research is not generally being accorded a high priority as compared with work in such fields as applied economics, demography and social administration. This comparative neglect is in ignorance of the kind of service anthropologists could give.

Looking forward, there are several directions in which social anthropology needs careful scrutiny and in which there are prospects of useful development. One is in the construction of *more problem-oriented research*. Hitherto social anthropology has had to concentrate upon blocking in large sectors of its field in order to obtain the proper ethnographic coverage and ensure that no significant variation in major institutional forms escaped its net. Increasingly attention has been devoted to more specific problems, for example, from the broad classification of types of marriage and of family to examination of the processes involved in the stability of marriage and in the development of the family cycle. But there is, nevertheless, still great need to narrow down research enquiries and pin-point specific problems, for formulation and testing of more exact hypotheses. Put another way, part of the job of social anthropology over the next ten years will be to identify the variables in a chosen social situation and isolate them as far as possible so that the effects of any one variable can be estimated.

This may also involve *more direction of research interests* of fieldworkers, focusing the energies of several different sectors of a common problem. The intimate personal character of much anthropological field enquiry does not lend itself easily to teamwork (apart from the husband-wife team, which has been long established as a very effective instrument for obtaining complementary field data). But *more use of co-ordinated field projects*, with a central supervisor guiding the field work of several individual research anthropologists, may be envisaged; as may more specific use of local field assistants

75

to gather a greater range of systematic quantifiable data.

Linked with closer problem-orientation is the need for *closer definition of the relations of social anthropology with other disciplines* such as economics and political science. In studies concerned with, for instance, indigenous political systems, the approaches of historians working on documentary sources and of social anthropologists working on the direct study of institutions have tended to converge. But in the fields of contemporary economic and political change the relationship is not yet so clear. Useful statistical surveys of communities or patterns of economic activity have sometimes been carried out by economists or by government agencies with little regard to their social context. This sets undue limitations on the value of the results. Similarly, analyses of the rise of new political parties in Africa and of other political developments have sometimes ignored the relevant materials on social structure made available by social anthropologists. Here, however, various important recent studies by political scientists have made full use of anthropological data, while anthropologists have shown familiarity with the concepts and problems of political science.

Interdisciplinary research is one way of meeting the problems indicated here, and this is favoured by a majority of social anthropologists. The need for special careful planning for such work is however stressed. It would seem that anthropologists with wide training (for instance, with some knowledge of demography, statistics, economics) are more likely to fit into such a scheme than those who lack acquaintance with such other social science disciplines. Where such familiarity is not provided at undergraduate level, it should be given at the postgraduate level. Again, experience shows that to be really fruitful, inter-disciplinary field research may require as much as six months of joint discussion and planning by the participants, preferably in or near the actual area of research. Moreover, such work needs regular support by the holding of interdisciplinary seminars or conferences, in which the individual research workers report on and discuss their work.

There seems to be a general view that social anthropology needs a more sophisticated scientific approach, with a *more precise formulation of hypotheses* for testing. One expression of this is the view that higher priority might be given in field research to projects for re-study of societies studied at an earlier date. Several such studies have already been made by British social anthropologists, and the results have been useful in providing measures of social and economic change. But such studies would undoubtedly benefit from closer attention to the problems to be examined, and from the prior formulation of hypotheses which could then be tested when in the field.

Another basic question facing social anthropology is that of the *balance between theoretical and applied research*. Clearly, social anthropologists as a whole are insistent on the continued necessity of basic research in their subject. But applied research has its place. Opinions as to the usefulness of social anthropologists as analysts or advisers on policy in practical situations vary considerably, and experiences in this field seem to have been very diverse. Degree of interest in theoretical or applied anthropology may be to a considerable extent a matter of personal temperament. But increasing precision in problem-oriented research and more effective isolation of relevant variables may be expected to give social anthropology a clearer role to play in applied fields. Experiments in applied anthropology (including some of those usually referred to as community development) provide utilizable data as evidence to test propositions in economic anthropology. It would also seem likely that as research in social anthropology becomes more a matter of public interest, with expenditure of public funds, the pressure for social anthropology to contribute where possible towards a solution of social problems will grow. Now it is clear that no applied science can flourish without an effective theoretical underpinning. This is particularly true of social anthropology, where the theoretical framework of the subject still demands a very great deal of systematic, intensive attention. But social anthropologists may be increasingly expected to consider how and in which field they can exercise their knowledge and skills on the applied side.

An argument is also strongly advanced in some quarters that the social anthropologist should make a special contribution in *'action-centred' research* of an interdisciplinary kind, where participant observation is not limited to observation alone, but includes intervention and role modification or change, directed at improvement in social relations. Those anthropologists who have carried out work of this kind understand its difficulties, but most feel that it can be of special value in the developing countries. Possibilities of short-term work with international agencies such as UNESCO and FAO should be explored, as offering opportunities to social anthropologists with expert knowledge of particular countries or areas.

5 Resources and Needs

Manpower

The established social anthropologists of Britain are a well-integrated group, and identification of them is relatively simple. Some social anthropology is taught in training colleges and schools, but little if any research is done from there; and while research students at universities make a considerable contribution to our knowledge of the subject, few are at the stage of full participation in the research effort. For planning, guidance, and conduct of research, and publication of the results, the effective body of social anthropologists is represented by the resident members of the Association of Social Anthropologists. Nearly all the members occupy posts in university departments of anthropology or sociology, although a significant few are engaged in research institutions, such as the Tavistock Institute and the Institute of Race Relations. The Association is a strictly professional one, normal qualifications being a training in the British tradition of social anthropology, a higher degree or significant publications in the subject, and a university or research institute post. It was founded in 1946 with about 20 members, and now has some 240 members. Although this more than tenfold increase over two decades illustrates the development of the subject, the numbers involved are still small (which makes the output of research and publications all the more creditable). Originally the Association was conceived in terms of Commonwealth membership, and nearly all the members are British, of various citizenship. A few social anthropologists from other countries, but with British affiliations, have been elected recently. At the present time approximately half the members of the Association are resident in Britain; the remainder are mainly in Commonwealth countries, with a significant minority (both British and American) in the USA.

An important implication of this distribution of membership is that of international traffic in ideas. Departments of social anthropology in Britain suffer individually, like all other university departments, when they lose members, as happens periodically, to another country. But the 'brain drain' in the past has operated very much to the benefit of Britain in social anthropology. Not only have British universities been helped to build up their resources by research students and staff from Commonwealth countries—five of the dozen or so professors in the UK are originally from abroad—but in the decade after the war a valuable contribution to research sponsored by Britain in African territories was made by anthropologists from the USA. A recent instance of this scholarly traffic was a conference in 1963 between members of the Association of Social Anthropologists and a group of American social anthropologists, when the interchange of ideas resulted in four volumes of papers on new approaches in the subject: *The Relevance of Models for Social Anthropology; Political Systems and the Distribution of Power; The Social Anthropology of Complex Societies;* and *Anthropological Approaches to the Study of Religion.*

From the comparative nature of its subject matter, social anthropology is one of the most internationally oriented of the social disciplines, and it is vital that the intellectual cross-fertilization this implies should be able to continue.

To estimate the number of British-based potential social anthropologists already undergoing research training is not easy. The available figures of postgraduates from departments do not always separate British from the rest, and it is not by any means clear what will be the proportion of those who will complete their research training. Yet again, some who are not British by origin may well become incorporated into the academic life of this country, as has happened in the past. But an informed guess which takes into consideration the total number of postgraduate students and the number of Ph.D.

registrations and reduces them according to the proportion of British students concerned (so far as this is known) gives a figure of rather less than 150 British postgraduate students in training. Of these not more than half are working for a doctorate or likely to proceed thereto. Allowing for wastage, and the length of time needed to complete field research and write up the results, probably not more than a dozen to a score of British social anthropologists carry their research training right through to doctoral completion in any year.

The question as to whether this supply is adequate to meet the research needs of the subject is simple to answer—it is not. But the question as to how to develop this research manpower more adequately is much more difficult. To some extent it is a question of finance, since our information suggests that more assured provision of funds for field research would attract more research workers. But the issue depends also on the kind of projection that is made about the future career structure of research workers in anthropology. At the present time virtually the only outlet for an anthropological research worker in Britain is in a university department. There is as yet no significant teaching of anthropology in schools or training colleges to serve as an employment backlog. Special institutes for social studies absorb a few, as also do market research and allied commercial operations. But there is no substantial development of posts in industry, such as is offered to economists and statisticians, to provide alternative avenues for income and research interests. Moreover, the attainment of independence by many overseas territories has meant some curtailment of employment opportunities, at least for British anthropologists in their institutes concerned with social research. Provision of employment for social anthropologists, therefore, as in fields where social administration and social welfare demand intensive studies of family structures, of minority groups, of housing problems and community living, seems highly necessary if provisions for increased research training are to be realistic and effective.

In this connection it is relevant to note that the problem of supply and demand in scientific manpower resources has been particularly acute in American anthropology in recent years. At least three Federal agencies have long had definite commitments to expand the output of anthropologists through various training and other programmes, and each of these agencies has been seeking valid data on which to base the justification for these programmes.[1]

Fieldwork needs

TASK

Fieldwork is a prime requirement in social anthropology. The emergence of the theoretical discipline was paralleled by the crystallization of more systematic methods of the collection of field data. As C. G. Seligman once wrote, fieldwork is to social anthropology what the blood of the martyrs is to the Church! To stress the prime importance of field research for the social anthropologist is not to undervalue the contribution of 'armchair anthropology'. But it has long been recognized that to obtain social data of the greatest relevance they must be collected in the field by trained research workers.

The significance of field research for social anthropology is threefold.

First, if, as is common practice, fieldwork is carried out in

---

[1] For the first time anthropologists in the United States were asked, in April 1966, to submit information about their training, interests, activities, and areas of specialization to the US National Sciences Register of Scientific and Technical Personnel. This register is handled by the National Science Foundation, co-operating with the various scientific societies. All anthropologists who have the Ph.D. in anthropology or its equivalent are included. (*A.A.A. Fellow Newsletter* vol. 7 no. 4, April 1966, p. 1.)

an alien society, it gives what Americans term 'exposure' to institutions and values different from those of the observer, and necessarily enforces a comparative viewpoint.

Second, it provides essential training in the conduct of personal relationships in interview and observation situations, in the exercise of responsibility for selection of problems and the methods to tackle them, and in the use of various techniques of systematic record.

Third, it provides the basis for contributions to ethnographic knowledge and to anthropological theory. In this connection it must be emphasized that even field research carried out by graduate students in a pre-doctoral phase can yield most valuable results. Some of the best known books in social anthropology have been the direct outcome of field research at this stage. (That research students in social anthropology often make an original contribution to knowledge should be borne in mind when provision for their fieldwork is considered.)

Anthropologists have written relatively little about their field methods by comparison, for example, with sociologists and psychologists. This is partly because of the intensely personal character of much anthropological field research, which makes it difficult to characterize method effectively except by extensive documentation. But some accounts have been given.

PROBLEMS OF INTERVIEW AND OBSERVATION

A modern social anthropologist tries to put himself in as close communication as possible with the people of the social unit or category he is studying. Much of his raw material consists of recorded linguistic statement. The collection of this assumes either a working knowledge of the vernacular language, or that the anthropologist acquires this during the course of his fieldwork. Nowadays all social anthropologists obtain some formal vernacular language training and/or instruction in linguistics before they engage in field research in an alien community. Such training is arduous and a matter of great importance. Where knowledge of the written as well as spoken language is required, for instance with Chinese or Malay, the training period should be calculated to allow for this. Experience seems to show that even where no training is obtained in the specific vernacular language in which anthropologists will work, study of the principles of language structure is an invaluable field aid.

Some social anthropologists have indicated that their command of the language, though quite adequate for everyday affairs, was imperfect in more technical occasions. This is a point which more anthropologists would do well to clarify, especially when they present interpretations of the beliefs or modes of thought of the people they have studied. Such analyses could often do with a much more systematic presentation of linguistic evidence over a wide range of contexts.

Linguistic material is obtained by a social anthropologist in three ways:

(a) recorded 'texts' taken down from an informant's dictation;
(b) statements noted during an interview or specific discussion;
(c) material jotted down while the anthropologist is present at some social event.

Each situation has its own particular problems. Those of the interview, common also to psychology and sociology, have received most attention outside social anthropology, and there is some case for more systematic attention to interview conditions by social anthropologists. Basic here are questions of selection and contextualization.

Fieldwork in social anthropology places great stress upon the importance of direct first-hand *observation* of behaviour. This is partly in order to correct the discrepancies of interpretation which may arise from reliance upon linguistic statement and interview techniques alone, and partly to compare actual with ideal patterns of behaviour.[1] The same problems of selection and interpretation of context arise in observational studies as in the collection of interview material. But when, as is normal, a social anthropologist spends upwards of a year or more living in the area concerned, his assumption is that his daily relations with the people will provide him with sufficient randomness of observation to minimize bias.

SPECIFIC METHODS

Specific field methods of social anthropology have been often described. No matter what the nature of the problem, some analysis of the structure of the society is normally a necessary precedent. Consequently, the regular field methods of the anthropologist include collection of genealogies, sociological census data, compilation of village plans, land-holding plans, etc. Systematization of field data to secure more reliable interpretation has been sought in various ways. Social anthropologists have tried to extend the scope of their case records. Gluckman and colleagues sponsored the 'extended case' method, and Turner has made valuable use of treatment of case material in 'social drama' terms, a method for the study of crises earlier employed by Hogbin. With the development of field methods, more specific quantitative studies have seemed necessary in order to be able to indicate more precisely regular patterns of behaviour and the range of variation from them. Statistical refinements such as tests of significance have sometimes been applied to quantitative material, but their aptness is still open to question.

Methods of random sampling have not been much used by social anthropologists in the collection of their material. The reasons are partly the physical difficulties of travel in rural

---

[1] Sophisticated survey research sometimes tests questionnaire answers by second, more intensive interviews, which may reveal discrepancies. A social anthropologist's first thought is usually to parallel questionnaire answers by some direct observation.

areas, partly the difficulty of gaining rapport with all communities and informants, and partly the difficulty in establishing a sampling universe with so many units of unknown quality. But some use of this procedure has been made, as by Fortes on the Ashanti Social Survey, by Mitchell and others in urban studies in Central Africa, or by Firth and colleagues in a recent study of kinship in North London.

Social anthropologists have traditionally done without elaborate surveys. But it seems likely that survey methods will become more and more necessary to comparative social anthropology, as:

(a) with an increasing body of background data on the societies of the world and an increasing understanding of their social and cultural systems, analysis is increasingly directed to more intensive studies of specific problems;

(b) with the posing of new types of problem there is need for new types of evidence;

(c) primitive 'societies' become integral parts of developing nations, and it no longer becomes possible to make assumptions of cultural homogeneity.

PHYSICAL AIDS

1. Documentary

Of growing importance to modern anthropological fieldwork is the use of documentary sources. This has been stimulated partly by the changing character of the anthropologist's problems, in which much greater emphasis now is laid upon social change and social development, and partly by the growing realization of the significance of the relation of social anthropology to historical studies. Anthropologists have always used published material, and the use of archives of governments, mission societies, etc. is well established. But clearly this is going to increase. In addition, as literacy spreads, anthropologists, who have used texts by literate informants and essays by schoolchildren in the past, will have to cope increasingly with the analysis of spontaneous documents written by members of the society studied. Such records, used as material for analysis of social situations rather than as a face-value account, can supplement the first-hand observations of the fieldworker. Informants who have been trained to keep specific routine records can also help to fill gaps in the anthropologist's experience and allow of analysis of much longer sequences than would be otherwise possible. (The case for employment of a literate member of the community studied as a research assistant is often very strong; for reasons given above, this applies to research students as well as to more senior workers.)

2. Linguistic
Development of tape recorders has given anthropological fieldworkers an invaluable aid. 'Texts' can be taken in full with the precise nuances used by the speaker, and sound records of social situations involving many participants can be made.

3. Photographic
For many years a camera has been a regular piece of apparatus needed by a fieldworker. Illustrations of social situations are an important part of anthropological publications, and photographs illustrating material culture obviate the necessity of a great deal of written description. Recently the use of film cameras has allowed record of 'action' situations.

The use of equipment such as tape recorders and cameras, especially film cameras, does however present some serious problems. The first problem is that of selection of material. A purist may argue that the tapes, films, and photographs brought back from an expedition are only a partial presentation of the life of the people, and reveal the anthropologist's bias rather than an objective account. This objection, however, which is basic to all field study, is one which the anthropologist can usually meet. The second problem is that of expenditure

R.S.A.—7   87 of time. Time is a fieldworker's scarce resource, and when he is occupied in the mechanics of sound recording or filming he cannot devote himself fully to his prime business of observation. The third problem, perhaps most serious of all, is that of analysis and publication of the results. Stills from photographs are readily made available by plates in books and articles; tape and film material is more difficult to display scientifically. As yet few systematic results have emerged from the considerable amount of such material that has been accumulated. The value of such aids would seem considerable, but we still have to work out techniques for their proper systematic utilization.

TREATMENT OF FIELD MATERIALS

Field notes have traditionally been regarded as the private resource of the individual anthropologist, disposed of at his discretion. Some fieldworkers, it is said, have even destroyed their notes when they have written up a subject for publication; others treat them as raw material of no evidential value. This is fundamentally unsatisfactory, and has led to the situation in which there are probably very few sets of original data for any of the classical field monographs available for consultation by scholars. The case for preservation of field notes is, first, that in most developing countries the rapidly changing situation makes it impossible for any later investigator to repeat the observations of his predecessor, and there is no way of testing the assertions made in printed form except by going back to the original notes. Second, these notes acquire a historical value, apart from any use to which the fieldworker may put them. For non-literate cultures, the anthropologist's record of customary law may in the long run have historical value for reconstruction of the past comparable to that of the Frankish codes or Anglo-Saxon wills. The amount of original interpretation that has gone into the working up of these notes may make it difficult to reconstruct the reasons why the final account assumed the particular form it did, but the problems involved are not unfamiliar to historians.

An implication from this is that the time has come for the establishment of a British anthropological archive, for the deposit of original field notes and ancillary materials (which could be sealed for a period of years where advisable).[1]

MODERN PROBLEMS

Apart from specific problems of improvement of field methodology and record practices, there are three broad questions in which social anthropologists are becoming increasingly involved.

(a) The position of the anthropological fieldworker is becoming one of increasing sensitivity as literacy spreads, and the people in the societies in which he customarily works read what he writes about them. Modern difficulties of carrying out field research, and even of obtaining entry to the field in some of the more sensitive political communities are well known. A stocktaking of the position here seems advisable. This has obvious international implications, since the record of one fieldworker may affect the prospects of others for perhaps a generation to come. This may mean in the long run the development of more carefully planned programmes of collective research, with agreement between major parties.

(b) Linked with this is the problem of the responsibility which the fieldworker has for his conduct and for his treatment of his field materials. Several senior anthropologists have analysed the ethical issues involved in the use of

---

[1] The Royal Anthropological Institute already has some materials of this kind, especially in the form of photographic data. The British Library of Political and Economic Science also has certain archival materials from anthropologists formerly associated with the London School of Economics, in particular B. K. Malinowski and S. F. Nadel.

field data revealing intimate aspects of the personality and history of people studied.[1]

(c) Another aspect of this major problem is the specific relation of the fieldworker to the people among whom he works as conditioning the quality and interpretation of his material. Emphasis laid upon 'value-free', 'problem-oriented', and 'committed' research will vary with the fieldworker. Some interesting accounts have been written of the involvement of the fieldworker with members of the communities he studies. But there is need for much more systematic description of fieldwork methods, including analysis of the role played by the anthropologist himself. It has been suggested that diaries may be useful in such assessment. It seems, however, from those of Malinowski's diaries which have recently been published that they are of help towards an understanding rather of the personality of the fieldworker than of his role in society.

The development of field research methods in social anthropology would seem to imply a need for greater clarification and more precise specification of problems for study, and greater systematization in the collection of material. This also implies a clearer statement of the anthropologist's own position in the total situation. But in the last resort fieldwork depends upon effective communication, and this is something which cannot be prescribed in rules.

General research resources

Provisions for consultation of relevant literature on the whole seem adequate for British social anthropologists. The magnificent library of the Royal Anthropological Institute is fairly easily available to most scholars, and the copyright university

---

[1] Another issue which has engaged the attention of American anthropologists recently is the attempted use of scientific research by governments for political ends, including the gathering of para-military intelligence and allied activities. Naturally, such political use of ostensibly by scientific research has been strongly condemned.

libraries are well stocked; but others still need strengthening· Research in a few special fields may require travel for consultation, for example anyone working on topics with Indonesian data will almost certainly need to visit the Netherlands.

There is a fairly general view that more provision needs to be made for *comparative* research in social anthropology. It is argued by some scholars that an attempt should be made to fill the gap by acquisition for Britain of a copy of the Human Relations Area File, a vast compendium of indexed materials from the peoples of the globe, produced from Yale. This has been used extensively by American scholars for comparative work, and a copy of the File at the Laboratoire d'Anthropologie Sociale in Paris has been available to Lévi-Strauss for his important general studies of myth. The data of this File are of uneven value, both its initial and its recurrent costs are considerable, and there is some question as to whether the methods of record and classification may not soon be superseded. But the question of provision for handling comparative problems where an extensive search for social correlates is involved needs serious consideration.

It is also suggested that there should be provision of counter-sorters and calculating machines in major departments of anthropology so that staff can process their own material and engage in comparative work. This would also allow of the training of students in more sophisticated techniques than at present—and the acquisition of techniques with maximum transfer value in the social sciences generally would be of benefit for interdisciplinary co-operation.

A suggestion has also been made that for maximum use, field notes of anthropologists should be coded in such a way as to facilitate comparative research. It is admitted that the attainment of this objective is probably still a long way off, but that as a step forward a tentative schema for classifying field data should be prepared. Individual initiative would be preserved since any worker could make his own additional headings, but such a schema would be a necessary preliminary to the more general use of field data for comprehensive comparison.

Other facilities which need improvement are those of photographic material and recorded sound. This is a branch of the subject which has been grossly neglected so far, by British anthropologists, particularly by comparison with American and European colleagues. More systematic attention to collection and analysis of film and tape materials for the study of ritual and other patterned social behaviour is particularly relevant, in view of the current interest of some social anthropologists in the work of ethologists.

The stress of British social anthropology upon the analysis of documentary materials obtained by first-hand observation of social behaviour has led to an undervaluing of objects of 'material culture'. At the moment, departmental collections of ethnographic objects are minimal and unsystematic, used only incidentally for teaching purposes and still less for research. Yet systematic study of such cultural material in relation to social behaviour opens up important problems of the relation of technology to social structure; the study of what has been conventionally called 'primitive art' is an obvious growing point here.

Financial considerations

It is not easy to arrive at a global figure of the costs of research in social anthropology undertaken from Britain in recent years. But it has been estimated from an enquiry in 1966 on the basis of returns from nearly half the members of the Association of Social Anthropologists that the total net cost of research (i.e. excluding salary in most cases) for all the 220 members has been of the order of £500,000 over the last five years. Taking only the 80 members based in this country, from a sample return from about three-quarters it can be said that *net* expenditure over the five years has been of the order of £200,000 to £225,000 or £40,000 to £45,000 per annum. From these returns it appears also that about two-thirds of the

British anthropologists spent some period in field research during the five years—often using a vacation for part of the time. On the average, this means a *net* expenditure of about £800 per head per annum for those who went to the field. British social anthropologists have an economical tradition in their field research—both in use of manpower and expenditure of money. But even then the sums needed to support this modest scale of field research are considerable.

It is to be noted also:

(a) that these amounts are *exclusive* of all university salaries, and exclude almost all salaries of those research workers on the staff of institutes;

(b) that the figures represent almost entirely the costs of *field* research; cost of documentary research, research assistance, preparation of manuscripts, etc., have certainly in many cases not been included in the returns;

(c) that these costs refer primarily to the research carried out by *established* workers, i.e. in university or comparable posts, and *not* to the mass of research investigations carried out by research students (in a few cases only, a person recently appointed to a post has included in the return his field costs incurred as a research student);

(d) expenditure on some large items of 'commissioned' research has not been included, for lack of information.

As regards sources of funds, a breakdown indicates approximately the following proportions of the total sum:

	%
Foundations	35
Governments and government agencies	35
Universities	18
International organizations, industry, personal contributions	12
All	100

Points to be made about this distribution are:

(a) British social anthropologists use a diverse range of sources to finance their research, for instance at least ten foundations provided support.

(b) While the contributions of foundations and of governments are about equal, and those of universities only half this, the former tend to be in larger grants. Universities have contributed to about half the research projects under consideration. The impression from the data obtained is that university aid has been sought wherever possible, that the universities have given what they could afford, but that they have been able to provide less than one-fifth of the sums required.

(c) British anthropological research has relied heavily over the past five years on foreign support. About 30 per cent of the total sums provided have come from abroad—about half the foundation grants in amount, one-third of the university grants and one-fifth of the government grants have come from foreign sources. The foreign foundation grants have come from the USA, the foreign government and university grants from the countries in which the anthropologists have worked. At least two of the grants came from the US National Science Foundation. There is reason to think that this and other American sources may not be so readily available as before.

(d) It is also worth noting that in nearly half the research projects the anthropologist made some personal contribution himself, either towards the field costs or, more usually, towards the cost of preparing the materials for publication. The amounts involved were in most cases small, and totalled only about 4 per cent of the total figure. But for some of these, usually junior, people such contributions have meant considerable sacrifice. There is undoubted need for provision for small-scale documentary research, and for the costs of preparation of field material for publication (including such items as drawing maps and diagrams, and printing photographs for illustration).

If a projection of research finance in social anthropology required from the SSRC over the next five years be attempted, something like the following emerges (if we make certain rather arbitrary assumptions[1]). Let us assume that support from British foundations and British universities continues at the present proportionate level, that support from American foundations and foreign governments and universities decreases by half, and that the SSRC takes over most of the finance previously found by British government departments (e.g. DSIR). Let us also assume that with the establishment of new posts in social anthropology, either alone or in departments of sociology, the research need among established anthropologists will rise by 20 per cent. Let us also assume that the need for postgraduate studentships for research, with consequent accruing field costs, will rise similarly. From university department estimates the average cost of a year's field research for a graduate student is at present around £1,500. By 1972 the budget for social anthropology should be in the region of:

(a) £50,000 per annum for staff research, made up by—

	£
British foundations	9,000
Other foundations	4,000
British universities	6,000
Other universities	1,500
Other governments, etc.	1,500
SSRC	28,000
All	£50,000

(b) £45,000 for *field* research of British graduate students—

---

[1] Figures do not allow for possible increased costs as a result of the devaluation of sterling.

of which the SSRC share is unlikely to be much less than £40,000 per annum.

An *average* figure of somewhere in the region of £65,000 to £70,000 per annum is therefore probable as a requirement for *SSRC support* of a realistic—i.e. conservative—British research programme in social anthropology for the next few years. (This does *not* include the cost of the research studentships for ordinary subsistence in Britain and fees.) This amount allows for only a small degree of escalation. A trend towards more concerted programmes of research, resulting in demands for substantial sums rather than for relatively small amounts in support of loosely related individual projects, is likely to increase the demand considerably.

The personal contribution to research costs referred to earlier is linked with the question of facilities for writing up field materials. There is a very strong indication that British social anthropologists feel that the present facilities available to them are far from being adequate, particularly for those (the majority) who combine a teaching post with research interests. Only one-third of the large section of anthropologists who gave opinion recorded their resources as satisfactory, and most of these were not university teachers, but research workers whose programme included time and facilities for writing up field materials.

Granted that shortage of time is an occupational disease of academics, there is still a very real problem here. There are two basic aspects of this problem: provision of time; and provision of facilities for general analysis of field data and for preparation (including typing) of manuscripts. Any lengthy period of anthropological field research usually yields a very substantial amount of original data, of theoretical as well as of descriptive ethnographic significance. It is clear that in most anthropological teaching departments there is a large mass of such research data waiting to be analysed and adequately written up. In institutes also there appears to be a tendency for research workers to become over-committed to field projects and not have sufficient time for writing up. There is thus a considerable salvage operation which should be undertaken if a great deal of labour and expense is not to go without proper return.

The profession has pointed out forcefully that there are two main categories of research worker needing help. One category is exemplified by the young postgraduate who has just completed his field research, and finds himself forced into taking a teaching appointment which allows inadequate time for working up his material. (Such a young anthropologist has reported that he cashed in his FSSU policy in order to obtain six months' writing-up time.) Solutions suggested here have been:

(a) to find finance for posts of research-assistant or research-associate type (which already obtain in some university departments), carrying a minimal teaching load and a definite prescription for writing up field data;

(b) to provide all recipients of SSRC field grants in social anthropology with a year's writing-up time at the end of the field period, on satisfactory evidence that the research had been adequately carried out. (Such provision was specifically available under the former Treasury studentships in foreign languages and cultures.)

The present SSRC studentship and fellowship programme is not adequate to cover this need. Many postgraduate students in social anthropology take a full three years to prepare for and carry out their field research, and an SSRC studentship cannot be extended for a fourth year when the writing up is usually carried out. Nor would such students be eligible for an SSRC fellowship, which is reserved either for post-doctoral students or for students converting from other disciplines. Moreover, many fourth-year students are by this time anxious to drop their status as students and begin their career within the university staff structure.

The other category of research anthropologist in need of assistance is the established teacher who, in vacation or on leave, carries out further field research but lacks time to prepare the results for publication. A solution suggested here is that teaching departments should be so organized or strengthened that members could be freed to undertake full-time research and writing up of materials on a rotational basis. Some departments already have such provisions; in others it would be possible to organize them. The provision of more research assistance could also help to speed up publication of results. Such assistance could also be used in rounding off a piece of fieldwork, since delays are sometimes due to lack of opportunity to collect final data.

A further suggestion, involving the social sciences as a whole, is that a research centre for advanced study might be established, comparable to the Palo Alto centre, though on a smaller scale, and financed independently of the universities. A number of British social anthropologists have received great benefit from the Palo Alto centre. An imaginative project of this kind might attract foundation assistance, especially if it would cater for some international scholars.

A sphere in which British social anthropologists could fruitfully engage more is in the combination of research abroad with a teaching post. More utilization is desirable here of the Ministry of Overseas Development's scheme for assisting UK departments by secondment arrangements to institutions in the developing countries.

There is no doubt that while the reputation of British social anthropology is high, British anthropologists are now at a disadvantage as regards overseas leave in comparison with their counterparts on the continent of Europe. A friendly director of a European research centre, in lamenting the lack of British scholars at his institution, has pointed out that the United Kingdom is seriously handicapped, by comparison with countries such as France, in respect of leave for university staff. Distinguished French scholars have been given leave at his centre for two, three or even four years, and at the end of what is conceived as a 'cultural mission' they return to their university. The State bears the cost of the scholar while he is abroad as a contribution to the *présence française*. French scholars of high calibre are thus enabled to teach and carry out research for long consecutive periods, thus not only becoming real specialists in their area of study but also impressing the character of French scholarship upon the country where they have chosen to undertake research. Because of security of tenure in their university and liberal emoluments provided by the State, such research workers abroad often come from senior as well as junior scholars, and thus carry with them the authority of French scholarship. French official and university institutions are very well organized for offering prompt technical assistance to foreign countries, for selecting scholars to carry out field research abroad, and for offering financial help to the cost of their field research. When research workers or teaching staff from the United Kingdom are needed, a variety of individual approaches has to be made, with delay and divided responsibility. Current or recent French practice should not necessarily be thought of as a perfect model by any means, but it does deserve closer study.

6 Conclusions

The Committee has regarded its function in this research review as that of exploring the field of social anthropology in general, and of setting out the range of problems and achievements, the broad limitations and needs of research, especially field research, in recent years.

The Committee wishes to draw attention to the following points:

(a) The *continuing need for theoretical research* in all major braches of social anthropology.

(b) The *need for support of new developments* in collaboration with research workers in a range of other subjects— e.g. classical scholars, linguists, philosophers, ethologists, population geneticists. The interdisciplinary relationships suggest significant new problems, and the variety of interests involved is symptomatic of an important trend in modern anthropological research which calls for special attention.

(c) Need for the *continuance of support for university-based research*. The most significant theoretical advances in social anthropology in Britain have, almost without exception, originated from research work sponsored by university departments.

(d) Provision for *the further systematic development of field research*. This is an essential prerequisite of both theoretical and ethnographic advance in British social anthropology. A basic contribution is made by field research to teaching in the subject. Field research is to the social anthropologist what the laboratory is to the natural scientist. But there is this important difference: the young field anthropologist, unlike the young natural scientist, rarely serves directly as an apprentice to a senior, more experienced, fieldworker. Individual field research, although often a gruelling experience, is an important part of the social anthropologist's training at the graduate stage; and communication of its results forms an essential part of the training of undergraduates. Hence, in this subject university teaching cannot be perpetuated unless there is continued field research by generations of fieldworkers.

(e) Specific recognition of the *original contribution to knowledge made by graduate students engaged in field research* as well as by more senior social anthropologists. Perhaps especially marked in social anthropology, this arises because of the great amount of ethnographic data still to be collected on structures, institutions, and beliefs over a wide variety of societies.

(f) The need for *more extended support of graduate students* engaging in field research. The special requirements of anthropological field research involve the student in a longer period of training than is customary in most other social sciences (normally four years).

(g) Advancement of the discipline depends upon comparative research of many kinds. But increasingly evident fields for research in social anthropology are offered by *developing societies and complex advanced societies*. As traditional societies are being modified and modernized by social, economic and political changes, the problems for social anthropological research are multiplied; the field is not restricted but widened.

(h) The *special contribution of social anthropology to the study of British society*. While social anthropology continues to need the stimulus of comparative studies, at the same time the intensive field techniques of the anthropologist can be fruitfully applied to the investigation of local communities and of institutional problems in ways which complement the studies of sociologists and other social scientists.

Divergent views are held about the problem of assigning priorities to different kinds of research in social anthropology.

Scarce resources may suggest the wisdom of giving preference to some types of research, or making special provision for some areas, for example relatively accessible locations in Britain and Europe. But the importance of safeguarding individual initiative in research is recognized as a prime requirement. Moreover, preservation of the comparative viewpoint in social anthropology requires freedom of the research worker to select the area most germane to his problem. One cannot tell in advance where pertinent theory may emerge, from what kinds of research the most fruitful leads may come. This argues for the advisability of not attempting to impose a directive on research energies by any prior general selection of problems or areas for preferred study, of people or departments for preferred support. At the same time, this does not rule out the possibility of focusing attention on a particular problem or field, as by the setting up of a research unit.

The Committee wishes to draw attention to the following points in particular, made in various contexts in this review:

(a) The need for encouragement of the use of more developed technical research apparatus. The fact that field research in social anthropology has been traditionally conducted in a remote, exotic environment has meant that the field-worker has normally been very self-reliant, making only minimal use of technical equipment. In recent years sophisticated technical apparatus has become increasingly portable. Electronic recording devices of all kinds, both visual and aural, are now much more reliable than in the past, and can be easily transported even to remote locations. There is need for systematic investigation as to how the traditional research methods of social anthropology can best be adapted to sophisticated technology of this kind. There is also need for careful investigation as to how far the analysis of existing ethnographic records can be improved by the use of data-processing equipment and computers. We also need to know how far future field research should be conducted in a more systematic way so as to allow for the handling of quantitative data on a comparative basis. Specific studies need to be undertaken on these points.

(b) Attention is directed to the problem of research archives. After nearly half a century of systematic field research in social anthropology a great mass of original field notes and other recorded data has accumulated, much of it still not properly preserved and collated. Such materials are now assuming the character of historical sources in the subject. The establishment of a British anthropological archive to house and handle such material is becoming urgent. Linked with this is the position of the Royal Anthropological Institute and its library. This Institute has already a unique collection of photographic and other anthropological materials, and its library especially has performed vital services for research in social anthropology. But these services, especially its archival facilities, need putting on an improved basis to allow them to operate effectively.

(c) On the manpower side adequate recruitment of suitable research workers in social anthropology depends upon the expansion of their career structure. The Heyworth Committee has pointed out that more established posts need to be created for persons qualified in the social science disciplines and trained in research methods: 'We wish to see a range of research posts in universities, units attached to universities, institutes outside universities, and government research establishments, subscribing to a common policy of interchangeability of pension rights and seniority grading and of secondments.'[1] With the growing interest in anthropological research in Britain, it

---

[1] *Report of the Committee on Social Studies* (HMSO, London, 1965) para. 115.

would seem that avenues of employment for social anthropologists might be sought outside university departments. In addition to looking to colleges of technology, anthropologists might seek posts as research analysts associated with hospitals, clinics, social welfare agencies, industrial enterprises. If social anthropologists and other social scientists were employed more widely in organizations of this kind, the findings of social science could influence action more directly.

(d) Provision needs to be made, as separate projects, for analyses of anthropological data already collected in the field. Field research in social anthropology is conducted with certain major theoretical problems in mind, but in the course of the field research a great amount of supplementary ethnographic data is usually recorded, leading to the consideration of a range of further problems. The immediate subject-matter of the enquiry is normally thoroughly analysed as part of the project, and published. But much additional field material has to await classification and analysis until the anthropologist can obtain the necessary funds for research assistance and preparation of results. This problem is especially acute with the younger anthropologists. It is paradoxical that it is relatively easy to obtain grants to undertake research but difficult to obtain adequate finance for the further analysis of research results. This is particularly the case where the research worker has begun to develop a line of enquiry after he has left the field, and wishes to re-work his field material for this purpose.

(e) Linked with this is the problem common to all social scientists of time for research. The Heyworth Committee has already pointed out[1] that the two functions of research and teaching in universities make competing demands for

---

[1] Op. cit., para. 14.

time. With social anthropologists this problem tends to assume, in particular, the form of need for time to work up material previously obtained in the field. There is a very real need to provide professional anthropologists with periods of time free from teaching duties to enable them to classify, analyse and prepare for publication the results of research for which the new data have already been collected.

(f) To aid in both the prosecution of research abroad by British social anthropologists and the dissemination of British scientific achievement and stimulus, facilities for combining research with teaching posts in foreign institutions should be extended. More concrete inducement is needed to British social anthropologists to undertake such work abroad, and to British universities to provide the requisite leave of absence.

SOME RECENT BRITISH WORK IN SOCIAL ANTHROPOLOGY

Publication of results of research is necessary if the material and ideas are to be made available to other research workers and people interested more generally. The total output of publication by British social anthropologists is considerable, comprising books and articles in many British and international journals. A complete bibliography of this recent work cannot be given here, but to give some idea of the range of topics and areas covered the following list sets out only books published between 1960 and 1967

1. ARDENER, E. W. *Divorce and Fertility: an African Study* (Oxford University Press, London, 1962)
2. ARGYLE, W. J. *The Fon of Dahomey* (Oxford University Press, London, 1966)
   ASSOCIATION OF SOCIAL ANTHROPOLOGISTS—monographs
3. (1) *The Relevance of Models for Social Anthropology* ed. M. Banton (Tavistock Publications, London, 1965)
4. (2) *Political Systems and the Distribution of Power* ed. M. Banton (Tavistock, London, 1965)
5. (3) *Anthropological Approaches to the Study of Religion* ed. M. Banton (Tavistock, London, 1965)
6. (4) *The Social Anthropology of Complex Societies* ed. M. Banton (Tavistock, London, 1965)
7. (5) *The Structural Study of Myth and Totemism* ed. E. D. Leach (Tavistock, London, 1967)
8. (6) *Themes in Economic Anthropology* ed. R. Firth (Tavistock, London, 1967)
9. BAILEY, F. G. *Tribe, Caste and Nation* (Manchester University Press, 1960)
10. BAILEY, F. G. *Politics and Social Change* (Oxford University Press, Berkeley, 1963)
11. BANTON, M. *Policemen in the Community* (Tavistock, London, 1964)
12. BANTON, M. *Roles: An Introduction to the Study of Social Relations* (Tavistock, London, 1965)

13. BANTON, M. *Race Relations* (Tavistock, London, Oct.–Nov. 1967)

14. BOISSEVAIN, J. *Saints and Fireworks: Religion and Politics in Rural Malta* (Athlone Press, London, 1965)

15. BURRIDGE, K. O. L. *Mambu: A Melanesian Millenium* (Methuen, London, 1960)

16. BUXTON, JEAN *Chiefs and Strangers: a Study of Political Assimilation Among the Mandari* (Oxford University Press, London, 1963)

17. CAMPBELL, J. K. *Honour, Family and Patronage: A Study of Institutions and Moral Values in a Greek Mountain Community* (Oxford University Press, London, 1964)

18. COHEN, A. *Arab Border-Villages in Israel* (Manchester University Press, 1965)

19. CUNNISON, I. *The Baggara Arabs* (Clarendon Press, Oxford, 1966)

20. CUNNISON, SHEILA *Wages and Work Allocation* (Tavistock, London, 1966)

21. DJAMOUR, JUDITH *The Muslim Matrimonial Court in Singapore* (Athlone Press, London, 1966)

22. DOUGLAS, MARY *Purity and Danger: An Analysis of Concepts of Pollution and Taboo* (Routledge & Kegan Paul, London, 1966)

23. DYSON-HUDSON, N. *Karimojong Politics* (Oxford University Press, London, 1966)

24. EPSTEIN, A. L. (ed.) *The Craft of Social Anthropology: A Study of Techniques of Field Workers* (Tavistock, London, Oct. 1967)

25. EPSTEIN, T. SCARLETT *Economic Development and Social Change in South India* (Manchester University Press, 1962)

26. EVANS-PRITCHARD, E. E. *Theories of Primitive Religion* (Oxford University Press, London, 1965)

27. FIRTH, R. *History and Traditions of Tikopia* (The Polynesian Society, Wellington, NZ, 1961)

28. FIRTH, R. *Tikopia Ritual and Belief* (Allen & Unwin, London, 1967)

29. FIRTH, R., and YAMEY, B. S. (eds.) *Capital, Saving and Credit in Peasant Societies* (Allen & Unwin, London, 1964)

30. FORTES, M. (ed.) *Marriage in Tribal Societies* (Cambridge University Press, London, 1962)

RESEARCH IN SOCIAL ANTHROPOLOGY

31. FRANKENBERG, R. *Communities in Britain* (Penguin, Harmondsworth, 1966)

32. FREEDMAN, M. *Chinese Lineage and Society: Fukien and Kwangtung* (Athlone Press, London, 1967)

33. GLUCKMAN, M. *Order and Rebellion in Tribal Africa* (Cohen & West, London, 1963)

34. GLUCKMAN, M. *Politics, Law and Ritual in Tribal Society* (Blackwell, Oxford, 1965)

35. GLUCKMAN, M. *The Ideas in Barotse Jurisprudence* (Yale University Press, 1965)

36. GLUCKMAN, M. (ed.) *Essays on the Ritual of Social Relations* by DARYLL FORDE and others (Manchester University Press, 1962)

37. GLUCKMAN, M. (ed.) *Closed Systems and Open Minds: The Limits of Naivety in Social Anthropology* (Oliver & Boyd, Edinburgh, 1964)

38. GOODY, J. *Death, Property and the Ancestors* (Tavistock, London, 1962)

39. GOODY, J. (ed.) *Succession to High Office* (Cambridge University Press, London, 1966)

40. GULLIVER, P. H. *Social Control in an African Society* (Routledge & Kegan Paul, London, 1963)

41. LEACH, E. R. *Rethinking Anthropology* (Athlone Press, London, 1961)

42. LEACH, E. R. *Pul Eliya: A Village in Ceylon—a Study of Land Tenure and Kinship* (Cambridge University Press, London, 1961)

43. LEWIS, I. M. *Islam in Tropical Africa* (Oxford University Press, London, 1966)

44. LIENHARDT, G. *Divinity and Experience: Religion of the Dinka* (Oxford University Press, London, 1961)

45. LITTLE, K. L. *West African Urbanization* (Cambridge University Press, London, 1965)

46. LITTLEJOHN, J. *Westrigg: The Sociology of a Cheviot Parish* (Routledge & Kegan Paul, London, 1962)

47. LLOYD, P. C. *Yoruba Land Law* (Oxford University Press, London, 1962)

48. LLOYD, P. C. (ed.) *New Elites in Tropical Africa* (Oxford University Press, London, 1966)

49. LLOYD, P. C. *Africa in Social Change* (Penguin, Harmonds-worth, 1967)

50. MAIR, LUCY P. *Primitive Government* (Penguin, Harmonds-worth, 1963)

51. MAIR, LUCY P. *New Nations* (Weidenfeld & Nicolson, London, 1963)

52. MAYBURY-LEWIS, D. *Akwê-Shavente Society* (Oxford University Press, London, 1967)

53. MAYER, A. C. *Caste and Kinship in Central India* (Routledge & Kegan Paul, London, 1960)

54. MAYER, A. C. *Peasants in the Pacific: A Study of Fiji Indian Rural Society* (Routledge & Kegan Paul, London, 1961)

55. MIDDLETON, J. *Lugbara Religion* (Oxford University Press, London, 1960)

56. NEEDHAM, R. *Structure and Sentiment: A Test Case in Social Anthropology* (Chicago University Press, 1962)

57. PATTERSON, SHEILA *Dark Strangers: a Sociological Study of the Absorption of a Recent West Indian Migrant Group in Brixton, South London* (Tavistock, London, 1963)

58. RICHARDS, AUDREY I. *East African Chiefs: a Study of Political Development in some Uganda and Tanganyika Tribes* (Faber, London, 1960)

59. RICHARDS, AUDREY I. *Chisungu: a Girls' Initiation Ceremony among the Bemba of Northern Rhodesia* (Faber, London, 1961)

60. ROSSER, C., and HARRIS, C. *The Family and Social Change* (Routledge & Kegan Paul, London, 1965)

61. SCHAPERA, I. *Praise Poems of Tswana Chiefs* (Oxford University Press, London, 1965)

62. SCHAPERA, I. (ed.) *Studies in Kinship and Marriage*—Dedicated to Brenda Z. Seligman (Royal Anthropological Institute, London, 1963)

63. SPENCER, P. *The Samburu: a Study of Gerontocracy in a Nomadic Tribe* (Routledge & Kegan Paul, London, 1965)

64. STIRLING, P. *Turkish Village* (Weidenfeld & Nicolson, London, 1965)

65. TURNBULL, C. M. *Wayward Servants* (Eyre & Spottiswood, London, 1966)

66. TURNER, V. W. *The Forest of Symbols: Aspects of Ndembu Ritual* (Cornell University Press, New York, 1967)
67. VAN VELSEN, J. *The Politics of Kinship* (Manchester University Press, 1964)
68. WORSLEY, P. *The Third World* (Weidenfeld & Nicolson, Chicago, 1964)